AETERNA PUBLISHING

2010

# Architects of Fate or,
# Steps to Success and Power

by

Orison Swett Marden

# TABLE OF CONTENTS

# PREFACE.

the demand for more than a dozen editions of "pushing to the front" during its first year and its universally favorable reception, both at home and abroad, have encouraged the author to publish this companion volume of somewhat similar scope and purpose. the two books were prepared simultaneously, and the story of the first, given in its preface, applies equally well to this.

inspiration to character-building and worthy achievement is the keynote of the present volume, its object, to arouse to honorable exertion youth who are drifting without aim, to awaken dormant ambitions in those who have grown discouraged in the struggle for success, to encourage and stimulate to higher resolve those who are setting out to make their own way, with perhaps neither friendship nor capital other than a determination to get on in the world.

nothing is so fascinating to a youth with high purpose, life, and energy throbbing in his young blood as stories of men and women who have brought great things to pass. though these themes are as old as the human race, yet they are ever new, and more interesting to the young than any fiction. the cry of youth is for life! more life! no didactic or dogmatic teaching, however brilliant, will capture a twentieth-century boy, keyed up to the highest pitch by the pressure of an intense civilization. the romance of achievement under difficulties, of obscure beginnings and triumphant ends; the story of how great men started, their struggles, their long waitings, amid want and woe, the obstacles overcome, the final triumphs; examples, which explode excuses, of men who have seized common situations and made them great, of those of average capacity who have succeeded by the use of ordinary means, by dint of indomitable will and inflexible purpose: these will most inspire the ambitious youth. the author teaches that there are bread and success for every youth under the american flag who has the grit to seize his chance and work his way to his own loaf; that the barriers are not yet erected which declare to aspiring talent, "thus far and no farther"; that the most forbidding circumstances cannot repress a longing for knowledge, a yearning for growth; that poverty, humble birth, loss of limbs or even eyesight, have not been able to bar the progress of men with grit; that poverty has rocked the cradle of the giants who have wrung civilization from barbarism, and have led the world up from savagery to the gladstones, the lincolns, and the grants.

the book shows that it is the man with one unwavering aim who cuts his way through opposition and forges to the front; that in this electric age, where everything is pusher or pushed, he who would succeed must hold his ground and push hard; that what are stumbling-blocks and defeats to the weak and vacillating, are but stepping-stones and victories to the strong and determined. the author teaches that every germ of goodness will at last struggle into bloom and fruitage, and that true success follows every right step. he has tried to touch the higher springs of the youth's aspiration; to lead him to high ideals; to teach him that there is something nobler in an occupation than merely living-getting or money-getting; that a man may make millions and be a failure still; to caution youth not to allow the maxims of a low prudence, dinned daily into his ears in this money-getting age, to repress the longings for a higher life; that the hand can never safely reach higher than does the heart.

the author's aim has been largely through concrete illustrations which have pith, point, and purpose, to be more suggestive than dogmatic, in a style more practical than elegant, more helpful than ornate, more pertinent than novel.

the author wishes to acknowledge valuable assistance from mr. arthur w. brown, of w. kingston, r. i.

o. s. m.

43 bowdoin st., boston, mass.

december 2, 1896.

# CHAPTER I.

## wanted--a man.

"wanted; men:
not systems fit and wise,
not faiths with rigid eyes,
not wealth in mountain piles,
not power with gracious smiles,
not even the potent pen:
wanted; men."

run ye to and fro through the streets of jerusalem, and see now, and know, and seek in the broad places thereof, if ye can find a man.--jeremiah.

all the world cries, where is the man who will save us? we want a man! don't look so far for this man. you have him at hand. this man,--it is you, it is i, it is each one of us! . . . how to constitute one's self a man? nothing harder, if one knows not how to will it; nothing easier, if one wills it.--alexandre dumas.

"'tis life, not death for which we pant!
'tis life, whereof our nerves are scant:
more life and fuller, that we want."

i do not wish in attempting to paint a man to describe an air-fed, unimpassioned, impossible ghost. my eyes and ears are revolted by any neglect of the physical facts, the limitations of man.--emerson.

but nature, with a matchless hand, sends forth her nobly born,
and laughs the paltry attributes of wealth and rank to scorn;
she moulds with care a spirit rare, half human, half divine,
and cries exulting, "who can make a gentleman like mine?"
eliza cook.

"in a thousand cups of life," says emerson, "only one is the right mixture. the fine adjustment of the existing elements, where the well-mixed man is born with eyes not too dull, nor too good, with fire enough and earth enough, capable of receiving impressions from all things, and not too susceptible, then no gift need be bestowed on him. he brings his fortune with him."

diogenes sought with a lantern at noontide in ancient athens for a perfectly honest man, and sought in vain. in the market place he once cried aloud, "hear me, o men;" and, when a crowd collected around him, he said scornfully: "i called for men, not pygmies."

the world has a standing advertisement over the door of every profession, every occupation, every calling; "wanted--a man."

wanted, a man who will not lose his individuality in a crowd, a man who has the courage of his convictions, who is not afraid to say "no," though all the world say "yes."

wanted, a man who, though he is dominated by a mighty purpose, will not permit one great faculty to dwarf, cripple, warp, or mutilate his manhood; who will not allow the over-development of one facility to stunt or paralyze his other faculties.

wanted, a man who is larger than his calling, who considers it a low estimate of his occupation to value it merely as a means of getting a living. wanted, a man who sees self-development, education and culture, discipline and drill, character and manhood, in his occupation.

a thousand pulpits vacant in a single religious denomination, a thousand preachers standing idle in the market place, while a thousand church committees scour the land for men to fill those same vacant pulpits, and scour in vain, is a sufficient indication, in one direction at least, of the largeness of the opportunities of the age, and also of the crying need of good men.

wanted, a man who is well balanced, who is not cursed with some little defect or weakness which cripples his usefulness and neutralizes his powers. wanted, a man of courage, who is not a coward in any part of his nature.

wanted, a man who is symmetrical, and not one-sided in his development, who has not sent all the energies of his being into one narrow specialty, and allowed all the other branches of his life to wither and die. wanted, a man who is broad, who does not take half views of things. wanted, a man who mixes common sense with his theories, who does not let a college education spoil him for practical, every-day life; a man who prefers substance to show, who regards his good name as a priceless treasure.

wanted, a man "who, no stunted ascetic, is full of life and fire, but whose passions are trained to heed a strong will, the servant of a tender conscience; who has learned to love all beauty, whether of nature or of art, to hate all vileness, and to respect others as himself."

god calls a man to be upright and pure and generous, but he also calls him to be intelligent and skillful and strong and brave.

the world wants a man who is educated all over; whose nerves are brought to their acutest sensibility, whose brain is cultured, keen, incisive, penetrating, broad, liberal, deep; whose hands are deft; whose eyes are alert, sensitive, microscopic, whose heart is tender, broad, magnanimous, true.

the whole world is looking for such a man. although there are millions out of employment, yet it is almost impossible to find just the right man in almost any department of life. every profession and every occupation has a standing advertisement all over the world: "wanted--a man."

rousseau, in his celebrated essay on education, says: "according to the order of nature, men being equal, their common vocation is the profession of humanity; and whoever is well educated to discharge the duty of a man cannot be badly prepared to fill any of those offices that have a relation to him. it matters little to me whether my pupil be designed for the army, the pulpit, or the bar. nature has destined us to the offices of human life antecedent to our destination concerning society. to live is the profession i would teach him. when i have done with him, it is true he will be neither a soldier, a lawyer, nor a divine. *let him first be a man*; fortune may remove him from one rank to another as she pleases, he will be always found in his place."

a little, short doctor of divinity in a large baptist convention stood on a step and said he thanked god he was a baptist. the audience could not hear and called "louder." "get up higher," some one said. "i can't," he replied. "to be a baptist is as high as one can get." but there is something higher than being a baptist, and that is being a *man*.

as emerson says, talleyrand's question is ever the main one; not, is he rich? is he committed? is he well-meaning? has he this or that faculty? is he of the movement? is he of the establishment? but is he anybody? does he stand for something? he must be good of his kind. that is all that talleyrand, all that state street, all that the common sense of mankind asks.

when garfield was asked as a young boy, "what he meant to be," he answered: "first of all, i must make myself a man, if i do not succeed in that, i can succeed in nothing."

montaigne says our work is not to train a soul by itself alone, nor a body by itself alone, but to train a man.

one great need of the world to-day is for men and women who are good animals. to endure the strain of our concentrated civilization, the coming man and woman must have an excess of animal spirits. they must have a robustness of health. mere absence of disease is not health. it is the overflowing fountain, not the one half full, that gives life and beauty to the valley below. only he is healthy who exults in mere animal existence; whose very life is a luxury; who feels a bounding pulse throughout his body, who feels life in every limb, as dogs do when scouring over the field, or as boys do when gliding over fields of ice.

pope, the poet, was with sir godfrey kneller, the artist, one day, when the latter's nephew, a guinea slave-trader, came into the room. "nephew," said sir godfrey, "you have the honor of seeing the two greatest men in the world." "i don't know how great men you may be," said the guinea man, "but i don't like your looks. i have often bought a much better man than either of you, all muscles and bones, for ten guineas."

sydney smith said, "i am convinced that digestion is the great secret of life, and that character, virtue and talents, and qualities are powerfully affected by beef, mutton, pie crust, and rich soups. i have often thought i could feed or starve men into virtues or vices, and affect them more powerfully with my instruments of torture than timotheus could do formerly with his lyre."

what more glorious than a magnificent manhood, animated with the bounding spirits of overflowing health?

it is a sad sight to see thousands of students graduated every year from our grand institutions, whose object is to make stalwart, independent, self-supporting men, turned out into the world saplings instead of stalwart oaks, "memory-glands" instead of brainy men, helpless instead of self-supporting, sickly instead of robust, weak instead of strong, leaning instead of erect. "so many promising youths, and never a finished man!"

the character sympathizes with and unconsciously takes on the nature of the body. a peevish, snarling, ailing man cannot develop the vigor and strength of character which is possible to a healthy, robust, jolly man. there is an inherent love in the human mind for wholeness, a demand that man shall come up to the highest standard; and there is an inherent protest or contempt for preventable deficiency. nature too demands that man be ever at the top of his condition. the giant's strength with the imbecile's brain will not be characteristic of the coming man.

man has been a dwarf of himself, but a higher type of manhood stands at the door of this age knocking for admission.

as we stand upon the seashore while the tide is coming in, one wave reaches up the beach far higher than any previous one, then recedes, and for some time none that follows comes up to its mark, but after a while the whole sea is there and beyond it, so now and then there comes a man head and shoulders above his fellow-men, showing that nature has not lost her ideal, and after a while even the average man will overtop the highest wave of manhood yet given to the world.

apelles hunted over greece for many years, studying the fairest points of beautiful women, getting here an eye, there a forehead and there a nose, here a grace and there a turn of beauty, for his famous portrait of a perfect woman which enchanted the world. so the coming man will be a composite, many in one. he will absorb into himself not the weakness, not the follies, but the strength and the virtues of other types of men. he will be a man raised to the highest power. he will be self-centred, equipoised, and ever master of himself. his sensibility will not be deadened or blunted by violation of nature's laws. his whole character will be impressible, and will respond to the most delicate touches of nature.

what a piece of work--this coming man! "how noble in reason. how infinite in faculties. in form and motion how express and admirable, in action how like an angel, in apprehension how like a god. the beauty of the world. the paragon of animals."

the first requisite of all education and discipline should be man-timber. tough timber must come from well grown, sturdy trees. such wood can be turned into a mast, can be fashioned into a piano or an exquisite carving. but it must become timber first. time and patience develop the sapling into the tree. so through discipline, education, experience, the sapling child is developed into hardy mental, moral, physical timber.

what an aid to character building would be the determination of the young man in starting out in life to consider himself his own bank; that his notes will be accepted as good or bad, and will pass current everywhere or be worthless, according to his individual reputation for honor and veracity; that if he lets a note go to protest, his bank of character will be suspected; if he lets two or three go to protest, public confidence will be seriously shaken; that if they continue to go to protest, his reputation will be lost and confidence in him ruined.

if the youth should start out with the fixed determination that every statement he makes shall be the exact truth; that every promise he makes shall be redeemed to the letter; that every appointment shall be kept with the strictest faithfulness and with full regard for other men's time, if he should hold his reputation as a priceless treasure, feel that the eyes of the world are upon him, that he must not deviate a hair's breadth from the truth and right; if he should take such a stand at the outset, he would, like george peabody, come to have almost unlimited credit and the confidence of all, and would have developed into noble man-timber.

what are palaces and equipages; what though a man could cover a continent with his title-deeds, or an ocean with his commerce, compared with conscious rectitude, with a face that never turns pale at the accuser's voice, with a bosom that never throbs with the fear of exposure, with a heart that might be turned inside out and disclose no stain of dishonor? to have done no man a wrong; to have put your signature to no paper to which the purest angel in heaven might not have been an attesting witness; to walk and live, unseduced, within arm's length of what is not your own, with nothing between your desire and its gratification but the invisible law of rectitude;--*this is to be a man.*

"he that of such a height hath built his mind,
and reared the dwelling of his thought so strong
as neither fear nor hope can shake the frame
of his resolved powers; nor all the wind
of vanity or malice pierce to wrong
his settled peace, or to disturb the same;
what a fair seat hath he; from whence he may
the boundless wastes and wilds of man survey."
[*lines found in one of the books of beecher's library.*]

a man is never so happy as when he is *totus in se*; as when he suffices to himself, and can walk without crutches or a guide. said jean paul richter: "i have made as much out of myself as could be made of the stuff, and no man should require more."

man is the only great thing in the universe. all the ages have been trying to produce a perfect model. only one complete man has yet been evolved. the best of us are but prophecies of what is to come.

what constitutes a state?
not high-raised battlement or labored mound,
thick wall or moated gate;
not cities proud with spires and turrets crowned;
not bays and broad-armed ports,
where, laughing at the storm, rich navies ride;
not starred and spangled courts,
where low-browed baseness wafts perfume to pride.
no: men, high-minded men,
with powers as far above dull brutes endued
in forest, brake, or den,
as beasts excel cold rocks and brambles rude,--
men who their duties know,

but know their rights, and knowing, dare maintain,
prevent the long-aimed blow,
and crush the tyrant while they rend the chain.
william jones.

god give us men. a time like this demands
strong minds, great hearts, true faith and ready hands:
men whom the lust of office does not kill;
men whom the spoils of office cannot buy;
men who possess opinions and a will;
men who have honor--men who will not lie;
men who can stand before a demagogue
and scorn his treacherous flatteries without winking;
tall men sun-crowned, who live above the fog
in public duty, and in private thinking.
anon.

open thy bosom, set thy wishes wide,
and let in manhood--let in happiness;
admit the boundless theatre of thought
from nothing up to god . . . which makes a man!
young.

"the wisest man could ask no more of fate
than to be simple, modest, manly, true."

in speech right gentle, yet so wise; princely of mien,
yet softly mannered; modest, deferent,
and tender-hearted, though of fearless blood.
edwin arnold.

# CHAPTER II.

## dare.

the spartans did not inquire how many the enemy are, but where they are.--agis ii.

what's brave, what's noble, let's do it after the high roman fashion, and make death proud to take us.--shakespeare.

better, like hector, in the field to die,
than, like a perfumed paris, turn and fly.
longfellow.

let me die facing the enemy.--bayard.

who conquers me, shall find a stubborn foe.--byron.

courage in danger is half the battle.--plautus.

no great deed is done
by falterers who ask for certainty.
george eliot.

fortune befriends the bold.--dryden.

tender handed stroke a nettle,
and it stings you for your pains;
grasp it like a man of mettle,
and it soft as silk remains.
aaron hill.

we make way for the man who boldly pushes past us.--bovee.

man should dare all things that he knows is right,
and fear to do nothing save what is wrong.
phebe cary.

soft-heartedness, in times like these,

shows softness in the upper story.
lowell.

o friend, never strike sail to fear. come into port grandly, or sail with god the seas.--emerson.

to stand with a smile upon your face against a stake from which you cannot get away--that, no doubt, is heroic. but the true glory is resignation to the inevitable. to stand unchained, with perfect liberty to go away, held only by the higher claims of duty, and let the fire creep up to the heart,--this is heroism.--f. w. robertson.

"steady, men! every man must die where he stands!" said colin campbell to the ninety-third highlanders at balaklava, as an overwhelming force of russian cavalry came sweeping down. "ay, ay, sir colin! we'll do that!" was the cordial response from men many of whom had to keep their word by thus obeying.

* * * * * *

"we have met the enemy and they are ours."

"he either fears his fate too much
or his deserts too small,
that dares not put it to the touch,
to gain or lose it all."

* * * * * *

"bring back the colors," shouted a captain at the battle of the alma, when an ensign maintained his ground in front, although the men were retreating. "no," cried the ensign, "bring up the men to the colors." "to dare, and again to dare, and without end to dare," was danton's noble defiance to the enemies of france.

"the commons of france have resolved to deliberate," said mirabeau to de breze, who brought an order from the king for them to disperse, june 23, 1789. "we have heard the intentions that have been attributed to the king; and you, sir, who cannot be recognized as his organ in the national assembly,--you, who have neither place, voice, nor right to speak,--you are not the person to bring to us a message of his. go, say to those who sent you that we are here by the power of the people, and that we will not be driven hence, save by the power of the bayonet."

when the assembled senate of rome begged regulus not to return to carthage to fulfill an illegal promise, he calmly replied: "have you resolved to dishonor me?

torture and death are awaiting me, but what are these to the shame of an infamous act, or the wounds of a guilty mind? slave as i am to carthage, i still have the spirit of a roman. i have sworn to return. it is my duty. let the gods take care of the rest."

the courage which cranmer had shown since the accession of mary gave way the moment his final doom was announced. the moral cowardice which had displayed itself in his miserable compliance with the lust and despotism of henry displayed itself again in six successive recantations by which he hoped to purchase pardon. but pardon was impossible; and cranmer's strangely mingled nature found a power in its very weakness when he was brought into the church of st. mary at oxford on the 21st of march, to repeat his recantation on the way to the stake. "now," ended his address to the hushed congregation before him,--"now i come to the great thing that troubleth my conscience more than any other thing that ever i said or did in my life, and that is the setting abroad of writings contrary to the truth; which here i now renounce and refuse as things written by a hand contrary to the truth which i thought in my heart, and written for fear of death to save my life, if it might be. and, forasmuch as my hand offended in writing contrary to my heart, my hand therefore shall be the first punished; for if i come to the fire it shall be the first burned." "this was the hand that wrote it," he again exclaimed at the stake, "therefore it shall suffer first punishment;" and holding it steadily in the flame, "he never stirred nor cried till life was gone."

"oh, if i were only a man!" exclaimed rebecca bates, a girl of fourteen, as she looked from the window of a lighthouse at scituate, mass., during the war of 1812, and saw a british warship anchor in the harbor. "what could you do?" asked sarah winsor, a young visitor. "see what a lot of them the boats contain, and look at their guns!" and she pointed to five large boats, filled with soldiers in scarlet uniforms, who were coming to burn the vessels in the harbor and destroy the town. "i don't care, i'd fight," said rebecca. "i'd use father's old shotgun--anything. think of uncle's new boat and the sloop! and how hard it is to sit here and see it all, and not lift a finger to help. father and uncle are in the village and will do all they can. how still it is in the town! there is not a man to be seen." "oh, they are hiding till the soldiers get nearer," said sarah, "then we'll hear the shots and the drum." "the drum!" exclaimed rebecca, "how can they use it? it is here. father brought it home last night to mend. see! the first boat has reached the sloop. oh! they are going to burn her. where is that drum? i've a great mind to go down and beat it. we could hide behind the sandhills and bushes." as flames began to rise from the sloop the ardor of the girls increased. they found the drum and an old fife, and, slipping out of doors unnoticed by mrs. bates, soon stood behind a row of sandhills. "rub-a-dub-dub, rub-a-dub-dub," went the drum, and "squeak, squeak, squeak," went the fife. the americans in the town thought that help had come from boston, and rushed into boats to attack the redcoats. the british paused in their work of destruction; and, when the fife began to play "yankee doodle," they scrambled into their boats and rowed in haste to the warship, which weighed anchor and sailed away as fast as the wind would carry her.

a woman's piercing shriek suddenly startled a party of surveyors at dinner in a forest of northern virginia on a calm, sunny day in 1750. the cries were repeated in quick succession, and the men sprang through the undergrowth to learn their cause. "oh, sir," exclaimed the woman as she caught sight of a youth of eighteen, but a man in stature and bearing; "you will surely do something for me! make these friends release me. my boy,--my poor boy is drowning, and they will not let me go!" "it would be madness; she will jump into the river," said one of the men who was holding her; "and the rapids would dash her to pieces in a moment!" throwing on his coat, the youth sprang to the edge of the bank, scanned for a moment the rocks and whirling currents, and then, at sight of part of the boy's dress, plunged into the roaring rapids. "thank god, he will save my child!" cried the mother, and all rushed to the brink of the precipice; "there he is! oh, my boy, my darling boy! how could i leave you?"

but all eyes were bent upon the youth struggling with strong heart and hope amid the dizzy sweep of the whirling currents far below. now it seemed as if he would be dashed against a projecting rock, over which the water flew in foam, and anon a whirlpool would drag him in, from whose grasp escape would seem impossible. twice the boy went out of sight, but he had reappeared the second time, although frightfully near the most dangerous part of the river. the rush of waters here was tremendous, and no one had ever dared to approach it, even in a canoe, lest he should be dashed to pieces. the youth redoubled his exertions. three times he was about to grasp the child, when some stronger eddy would toss it from him. one final effort he makes; the child is held aloft by his strong right arm, but a cry of horror bursts from the lips of every spectator as boy and man shoot over the falls and vanish in the seething waters below.

"there they are!" shouted the mother a moment later, in a delirium of joy. "see! they are safe! great god, i thank thee!" and sure enough they emerged unharmed from the boiling vortex, and in a few minutes reached a low place in the bank and were drawn up by their friends, the boy senseless, but still alive, and the youth almost exhausted. "god will give you a reward," solemnly spoke the grateful woman. "he will do great things for you in return for this day's work, and the blessings of thousands besides mine will attend you."

the youth was george washington.

"your grace has not the organ of animal courage largely developed," said a phrenologist, who was examining wellington's head. "you are right," replied the iron duke, "and but for my sense of duty i should have retreated in my first fight." that first fight, on an indian field, was one of the most terrible on record.

in the reverses which followed napoleon, he met the allies at arcis. a live shell having fallen in front of one of his young battalions, which recoiled and wavered in expectation of an explosion, napoleon, to reassure them, spurred his charger toward the instrument of destruction, made him smell the burning match, waited unshaken for the explosion, and was blown up. rolling in the dust with his mutilated steed, and rising without a wound amid the plaudits of his soldiers, he calmly called for another horse, and continued to brave the grape-shot, and to fly into the thickest of the battle.

when general jackson was a judge and was holding court in a small settlement, a border ruffian, a murderer and desperado, came into the court-room with brutal violence and interrupted the court. the judge ordered him to be arrested. the officer did not dare to approach him. "call a posse," said the judge, "and arrest him." but they also shrank in fear from the ruffian. "call me, then," said jackson; "this court is adjourned for five minutes." he left the bench, walked straight up to the man, and with his eagle eye actually cowed the ruffian, who dropped his weapons, afterwards saying, "there was something in his eye i could not resist."

one of the last official acts of the late president carnot, of france, was the sending of a medal of the french legion of honor to a little american girl, who lives in indiana. while a train on the pan handle railroad, having on board several distinguished frenchmen, was bound to chicago and the world's fair, jennie carey, who was then ten years old, discovered that a trestle was on fire, and that if the train, which was nearly due, entered it a dreadful wreck would take place. thereupon she ran out upon the track to a place where she could be seen from some little distance. then she took off her red flannel skirt and, when the train came in view, waved it back and forth across the track. it was seen, and the train stopped. on board of it were seven hundred people, many of whom must have suffered death but for jennie's courage and presence of mind. when they returned to france, the frenchmen brought the occurrence to the notice of president carnot, and the result was the sending of the medal of this famous french society, the purpose of which is the honoring of bravery and merit, wherever they may be found.

after the battle of fort donelson, the wounded were hauled down the hill in rough board wagons, and most of them died before they reached st. louis. one blue-eyed boy of nineteen, with both arms and both legs shattered, had lain a long time and was neglected. he said, "why, you see they couldn't stop to bother with us because they had to take the fort. when they took it we all forgot our sufferings and shouted for joy, even to the dying."

louis ix. of france was captured by the turks at the battle of mansoora, during the seventh crusade, and his wife marguerite, with a babe at the breast, was in damietta, many miles away. the infidels surrounded the city, and pressed the garrison so hard that it was decided to capitulate. the queen summoned the knights, and told them that she at least would die in armor upon the ramparts before the enemy should become masters of damietta.

"before her words they thrilled like leaves
when winds are in the wood;
and a deepening murmur told of men
roused to a loftier mood."

grasping lance and shield, they vowed to defend their queen and the cross to the last. damietta was saved.

pyrrhus marched to sparta to reinstate the deposed cleonymus, and quietly pitched his tents before laconia, not anticipating resistance. in consternation, the spartans in council decided to send their women to crete for safety. but the women met and asked queen archidamia to remonstrate. she went to the council, sword in hand, and told the men that their wives did not care to live after sparta was destroyed.

"we are brave men's mothers, and brave men's wives;
we are ready to do and dare;
we are ready to man your walls with our lives,
and string your bows with our hair."

they hurried to the walls and worked all night, aiding the men in digging trenches. when pyrrhus attacked the city next day, his repulse was so emphatic that he withdrew from laconia.

charles v. of spain passed through thuringia in 1547, on his return to swabia after the battle of muehlburg. he wrote to catherine, countess dowager of schwartzburg, promising that her subjects should not be molested in their persons or property if they would supply the spanish soldiers with provisions at a reasonable price. on approaching eudolstadt, general alva and prince henry of brunswick, with his sons, invited themselves, by a messenger sent forward, to breakfast with the countess, who had no choice but to ratify so delicate a request from the commander of an army. just as the guests were seated at a generous repast, the countess was called from the hall and told that the spaniards were using violence and driving away the cattle of the peasants.

quietly arming all her retinue, she bolted and barred all the gates and doors of the castle, and returned to the banquet to complain of the breach of faith. general alva told her that such was the custom of war, adding that such trifling disorders were not to be heeded. "that we shall presently see," said catharine; "my poor subjects must have their own again, or, as god lives, prince's blood for oxen's blood!" the doors were opened, and armed men took the places of the waiters behind the chairs of the guests. henry changed color; then, as the best way out of a bad scrape, laughed loudly, and ended by praising the splendid acting of his hostess, and promising that alva should order the cattle restored at once. not until a courier returned, saying that the order had been obeyed, and all damages settled satisfactorily, did the armed waiters leave. the countess then thanked her guests for the honor they had done her castle, and they retired with protestations of their distinguished consideration.

it was the heroic devotion of an indian girl that saved the life of captain john smith, when the powerful king powhatan had decreed his death. ill could the struggling colony spare him at that time.

when the consul shouted that the bridge was tottering, lartius and herminius sought safety in flight. but horatius strode still nearer the foe, the single champion of his country and liberty, and dared the ninety thousand to come on. dead stillness fell upon the tuscans, so astonished were they at the audacity of the roman. he first broke the awful silence, so deep that his clear, strong voice could be heard by thousands in both armies, between which rolled the tiber, as he denounced the baseness and perfidy of the invaders. not until his words were drowned by the loud crash of fiercely disrupturing timbers, and the sullen splash of the dark river, did his enemies hurl their showers of arrows and javelins. then, dexterously warding off the missiles with his shield, he plunged into the tiber. although stabbed in the hip by a tuscan spear which lamed him for life, he swam in safety to rome.

"it is a bad omen," said eric the red, when his horse slipped and fell on the way to his ship, moored on the coast of greenland, in readiness for a voyage of discovery. "ill-fortune would be mine should i dare venture now upon the sea." so he returned to his house, but his young son leif decided to go, and, with a crew of thirty-five men, sailed southward in search of the unknown shore upon which captain biarni had been driven by a storm, while sailing in another viking ship two or three years before. the first land that they saw was probably labrador, a barren, rugged plain. leif called this country heluland, or the land of flat stones. sailing onward many days, he came to a low, level coast thickly covered with woods, on account of which he called the country markland, probably the modern nova scotia. sailing onward, they came to an island which they named vinland on account of the abundance of delicious wild grapes in the woods. this was in the year 1000. here where the city of newport, r. i., stands, they spent many months, and then returned to greenland with their vessel loaded with grapes and strange kinds of wood. the voyage was successful, and no doubt eric was sorry he had been frightened by the bad omen.

may 10, 1796, napoleon carried the bridge at lodi, in the face of the austrian batteries. fourteen cannon--some accounts say thirty--were trained upon the french end of the structure. behind them were six thousand troops. napoleon massed four thousand grenadiers at the head of the bridge, with a battalion of three hundred carbineers in front. at the tap of the drum the foremost assailants wheeled from the cover of the street wall under a terrible hail of grape and canister, and attempted to pass the gateway to the bridge. the front ranks went down like stalks of grain before a reaper; the column staggered and reeled backward, and the valiant grenadiers were appalled by the task before them. without a word or a look of reproach, napoleon placed himself at their head, and his aids and generals rushed to his side. forward again, this time over heaps of dead that choked the passage, and a quick run, counted by seconds only, carried the column across two hundred yards of clear space, scarcely a shot from the austrians taking effect beyond the point where the platoons wheeled for the first leap. so sudden and so miraculous was it all that the austrian artillerists abandoned their guns instantly, and their supports fled in a panic instead of rushing to the front and meeting the french onslaught. this napoleon had counted on in making the bold attack. the contrast between napoleon's slight figure and the massive grenadiers suggested the nickname "little corporal."

the great secret of the success of joan of arc was the boldness of her attacks.

when stephen of colonna fell into the hands of base assailants, and they asked him in derision, "where is now your fortress?" "here," was his bold reply, placing his hand upon his heart.

it was after the mexican war when general mcclellan was employed as a topographical engineer in surveying the pacific coast. from his headquarters at vancouver he had gone south to the columbia river with two companions, a soldier and a servant. one evening he received word that the chiefs of the columbia river tribes desired to confer with him. from the messenger's manner he suspected that the indians meant mischief. he warned his companions that they must be ready to leave camp at a moment's notice. mounting his horse, he rode boldly into the indian village. about thirty chiefs were holding council. mcclellan was led into the circle, and placed at the right hand of saltese. he was familiar with the chinook jargon, and could understand every word spoken in the council. saltese made known the grievance of the tribes. two indians had been captured by a party of white pioneers and hanged for theft. retaliation for this outrage seemed indispensable. the chiefs pondered long, but had little to say. mcclellan had been on friendly terms with them, and was not responsible for the forest executions. still, he was a white man, and the chiefs had vowed vengeance against the race. the council was prolonged for hours before sentence was passed, and then saltese, in the name of the head men of the tribes, decreed that mcclellan should immediately be put to death in retaliation for the hanging of the two indian thieves.

mcclellan had said nothing. he had known that argument and pleas for justice or mercy would be of no avail. he had sat motionless, apparently indifferent to his fate. by his listlessness he had thrown his captors off their guard. when the sentence was passed he acted like a flash. flinging his left arm around the neck of saltese, he whipped out his revolver and held it close to the chief's temple. "revoke that sentence, or i shall kill you this instant!" he cried, with his fingers clicking the trigger. "i revoke it!" exclaimed saltese, fairly livid from fear. "i must have your word that i can leave this council in safety." "you have the word of saltese," was the quick response. mcclellan knew how sacred was the pledge which he had received. the revolver was lowered. saltese was released from the embrace of the strong arm. mcclellan strode out of the tent with his revolver in his hand. not a hand was raised against him. he mounted his horse and rode to his camp, where his two followers were ready to spring into the saddle and to escape from the villages. he owed his life to his quickness of perception, and to his accurate knowledge of indian character.

in 1866, rufus choate spoke to an audience of nearly five thousand in lowell in favor of the candidacy of james buchanan for the presidency. the floor of the great hall began to sink, settling more and more as he proceeded with his address, until a sound of cracking timber below would have precipitated a stampede with fatal results but for the coolness of b. f. butler, who presided. telling the people to remain quiet, he said that he would see if there were any cause for alarm. he found the supports of the floor in so bad a condition that the slightest applause would be likely to bury the audience in the ruins of the building. returning rather leisurely to the platform, he whispered to choate as he passed, "we shall all be in ---- in five minutes," then he told the crowd that there was no immediate danger if they would slowly disperse, although he thought it prudent to adjourn to a place where there would be no risk whatever. the post of danger, he added, was on the platform, which was most weakly supported, therefore he and those with him would be the last to leave. no doubt many lives were saved by his coolness.

many distinguished foreign and american statesmen were present at a fashionable dinner party where wine was freely poured, but schuyler colfax, then vice-president of the united states, declined to drink from a proffered cup. "colfax dares not drink," sneered a senator who had already taken too much. "you are right," said the vice-president, "i dare not."

when grant was in houston several years ago, he was given a rousing reception. naturally hospitable, and naturally inclined to like a man of grant's make-up, the houstonites determined to go beyond any other southern city in the way of a banquet and other manifestations of their good-will and hospitality. they made great preparations for the dinner, the committee taking great pains to have the finest wines that could be procured for the table that night. when the time came to serve the wine, the head-waiter went first to grant. without a word the general quietly turned down all the glasses at his plate. this movement was a great surprise to the texans, but they were equal to the occasion. without a single word being spoken, every man along the line of the long tables turned his glasses down, and there was not a drop of wine taken that night.

a deep sewer at noyon, france, had been opened for repairs, and carelessly left at night without covering or lights to warn people of danger. late at night four men stumbled in, and lay some time before their situation was known in the town. no one dared go to the aid of the men, then unconscious from breathing noxious gases, except catherine vassen, a servant girl of eighteen. she insisted on being lowered at once. fastening a rope around two of the men, she aided in raising them and restoring them to consciousness. descending again, she had just tied a rope around a third man, when she felt her breath failing. tying another rope to her long, curly hair, she swooned, but was drawn up with the man, to be quickly revived by fresh air and stimulants. the fourth man was dead when his body was pulled up, on account of the delay from the fainting of catherine.

two french officers at waterloo were advancing to charge a greatly superior force. one, observing that the other showed signs of fear, said, "sir, i believe you are frightened." "yes, i am," was the reply, "and if you were half as much frightened, you would run away."

"that's a brave man," said wellington, when he saw a soldier turn pale as he marched against a battery; "he knows his danger, and faces it."

"there are many cardinals and bishops at worms," said a friend to luther, "and they will burn your body to ashes as they did that of john huss." luther replied: "although they should make a fire that should reach from worms to wittenberg, and that should flame up to heaven, in the lord's name i would pass through it and appear before them." he said to another: "i would enter worms though there were as many devils there as there are tiles upon the roofs of the houses." another said: "duke george will surely arrest you." he replied: "it is my duty to go, and i will go, though it rain duke georges for nine days together."

"here i stand, i cannot do otherwise, god help me," exclaimed luther at the diet of worms, facing his foes.

a western paper recently invited the surviving union and confederate officers to give an account of the bravest act observed by each during the civil war. colonel thomas w. higginson said that at a dinner at beaufort, s. c., where wine flowed freely and ribald jests were bandied, dr. miner, a slight, boyish fellow who did not drink, was told that he could not go until he had drunk a toast, told a story, or sung a song. he replied: "i cannot sing, but i will give a toast, although i must drink it in water. it is 'our mothers.'" the men were so affected and ashamed that some took him by the hand and thanked him for displaying courage greater than that required to walk up to the mouth of a cannon.

it took great courage for the commercial quaker, john bright, to espouse a cause which called down upon his head the derision and scorn and hatred of the parliament. for years he rested under a cloud of obloquy, but bright was made of stern stuff. it was only his strength of character and masterly eloquence, which saved him from political annihilation. to a man who boasted that his ancestors came over with the conquerors, he replied, "i never heard that they did anything else." a tory lordling said, when bright was ill, that providence had inflicted upon bright, for the measure of his talents, disease of the brain. when bright went back into the commons he replied: "this may be so, but it will be some consolation to the friends and family of the noble lord to know that that disease is one which even providence cannot inflict upon him."

"when a resolute young fellow steps up to the great bully, the world, and takes him boldly by the beard," says holmes, "he is often surprised to find it come off in his hand, and that it was only tied on to scare away timid adventurers."

it takes courage for a young man to stand firmly erect while others are bowing and fawning for praise and power. it takes courage to wear threadbare clothes while your comrades dress in broadcloth. it takes courage to remain in honest poverty when others grow rich by fraud. it takes courage to say "no" squarely when those around you say "yes." it takes courage to do your duty in silence and obscurity while others prosper and grow famous although neglecting sacred obligations. it takes courage to unmask your true self, to show your blemishes to a condemning world, and to pass for what you really are.

it takes courage and pluck to be outvoted, beaten, laughed at, scoffed, ridiculed, derided, misunderstood, misjudged, to stand alone with all the world against you, but

"they are slaves who dare not be
in the right with two or three."

"there is never wanting a dog to bark at you."

"an honest man is not the worse because a dog barks at him."

"let any man show the world that he feels
afraid of its bark, and 'twill fly at his heels.
let him fearlessly face it, 't will leave him alone,
and 't will fawn at his feet if he fling it a bone."

we live ridiculously for fear of being thought ridiculous.

"'tis he is the coward who proves false to his vows,
to his manhood, his honor, for a laugh or a sneer:
'tis he is the hero who stands firm, though alone,
for the truth and the right without flinching or fear."

the youth who starts out by being afraid to speak what he thinks will usually end by being afraid to think what he wishes.

how we shrink from an act of our own. we live as others live. custom or fashion dictates, or your doctor or minister, and they in turn dare not depart from their schools. dress, living, servants, carriages, everything must conform, or be ostracized. who dares conduct his household or business affairs in his own way, and snap his fingers at dame grundy?

many a man has marched up to the cannon's mouth in battle who dared not face public opinion or oppose mrs. grundy.

it takes courage for a public man not to bend the knee to popular prejudice. it takes courage to refuse to follow custom when it is injurious to his health and morals. to espouse an unpopular cause in congress requires more courage than to lead a charge in battle. how much easier for a politician to prevaricate and dodge an issue than to stand squarely on his feet like a man.

as a rule, eccentricity is a badge of power, but how many women would not rather strangle their individuality than be tabooed by mrs. grundy? yet fear is really the only thing to fear.

"whoever you may be," said sainte-beuve, "great genius, distinguished talent, artist honorable or amiable, the qualities for which you deserve to be praised will all be turned against you. were you a virgil, the pious and sensible singer *par excellence*, there are people who will call you an effeminate poet. were you a horace, there are people who will reproach you with the very purity and delicacy of your taste. if you were a shakespeare, some one will call you a drunken savage. if you were a goethe, more than one pharisee will proclaim you the most selfish of egotists."

as the strongest man has a weakness somewhere, so the greatest hero is a coward somewhere. peter was courageous enough to draw his sword to defend his master, but he could not stand the ridicule and the finger of scorn of the maidens in the high priest's hall, and he actually denied even the acquaintance of the master he had declared he would die for.

"i will take the responsibility," said andrew jackson, on a memorable occasion, and his words have become proverbial. not even congress dared to oppose the edicts of john quincy adams.

if a man would accomplish anything in this world, he must not be afraid of assuming responsibilities. of course it takes courage to run the risk of failure, to be subjected to criticism for an unpopular cause, to expose one's self to the shafts of everybody's ridicule, but the man who is not true to himself, who cannot carry out the sealed orders placed in his hands at his birth, regardless of the world's yes or no, of its approval or disapproval, the man who has not the courage to trace the pattern of his own destiny, which no other soul knows but his own, can never rise to the true dignity of manhood. all the world loves courage; youth craves it; they want to hear about it, they want to read about it. the fascination of the "blood and thunder" novels and of the cheap story papers for youth are based upon this idea of courage. if the boys cannot get the real article, they will take a counterfeit.

don't be like uriah heep, begging everybody's pardon for taking the liberty of being in the world. there is nothing attractive in timidity, nothing lovable in fear. both are deformities and are repulsive. manly courage is dignified and graceful. the worst manners in the world are those of persons conscious "of being beneath their position, and trying to conceal it or make up for it by style."

bruno, condemned to be burned alive in rome, said to his judge: "you are more afraid to pronounce my sentence than i am to receive it." anne askew, racked until her bones were dislocated, never flinched, but looked her tormentor calmly in the face and refused to abjure her faith.

"we are afraid of truth, afraid of fortune, afraid of death, and afraid of each other." "half a man's wisdom goes with his courage," said emerson. physicians used to teach that courage depends on the circulation of the blood in the arteries, and that during passion, anger, trials of strength, wrestling or fighting, a large amount of blood is collected in the arteries, and does not pass to the veins. a strong pulse is a fortune in itself.

"rage," said shaftesbury, "can make a coward forget himself and fight."

"i should have thought fear would have kept you from going so far," said a relative who found the little boy nelson wandering a long distance from home. "fear?" said the future admiral, "i don't know him."

"doubt indulged becomes doubt realized." to determine to do anything is half the battle. "to think a thing is impossible is to make it so." *courage is victory, timidity is defeat.*

that simple shepherd-lad, david, fresh from his flocks, marching unattended and unarmed, save with his shepherd's staff and sling, to confront the colossal goliath with his massive armor, is the sublimest audacity the world has ever seen.

"dent, i wish you would get down, and see what is the matter with that leg there," said grant, when he and colonel dent were riding through the thickest of a fire that had become so concentrated and murderous that his troops had all been driven back. "i guess looking after your horse's legs can wait," said dent; "it is simply murder for us to sit here." "all right," said grant, "if you don't want to see to it, i will." he dismounted, untwisted a piece of telegraph wire which had begun to cut the horse's leg, examined it deliberately, and climbed into his saddle. "dent," said he, "when you've got a horse that you think a great deal of, you should never take any chances with him. if that wire had been left there for a little time longer he would have gone dead lame, and would perhaps have been ruined for life."

wellington said that at waterloo the hottest of the battle raged round a farmhouse, with an orchard surrounded by a thick hedge, which was so important a point in the british position that orders were given to hold it at any hazard or sacrifice. at last the powder and ball ran short and the hedges took fire, surrounding the orchard with a wall of flame. a messenger had been sent for ammunition, and soon two loaded wagons came galloping toward the farmhouse. "the driver of the first wagon, with the reckless daring of an english boy, spurred his struggling and terrified horses through the burning heap; but the flames rose fiercely round, and caught the powder, which exploded in an instant, sending wagon, horses, and rider in fragments into the air. for an instant the driver of the second wagon paused, appalled by his comrade's fate; the next, observing that the flames, beaten back for the moment by the explosion, afforded him one desperate chance, sent his horses at the smouldering breach and, amid the deafening cheers of the garrison, landed his terrible cargo safely within. behind him the flames closed up, and raged more fiercely than ever."

at the battle of friedland a cannon-ball came over the heads of the french soldiers, and a young soldier instinctively dodged. napoleon looked at him and smilingly said: "my friend, if that ball were destined for you, though you were to burrow a hundred feet under ground it would be sure to find you there."

when the mine in front of petersburg was finished, the fuse was lighted, and the union troops were drawn up ready to charge the enemy's works as soon as the explosion should make a breach. but seconds, minutes, and tens of minutes passed, without a sound from the mine, and the suspense became painful. lieutenant doughty and sergeant kees volunteered to examine the fuse. through the long subterranean galleries they hurried in silence, not knowing but they were advancing to a horrible death. they found the defect, fired the train anew, and soon a terrible upheaval of earth gave the signal to march to victory.

at the battle of copenhagen, as nelson walked the deck slippery with blood and covered with the dead, he said: "this is warm work, and this day may be the last to any of us in a moment. but, mark me, i would not be elsewhere for thousands." at the battle of trafalgar, when nelson was shot and was being carried below, he covered his face, that those fighting might not know their chief had fallen.

in a skirmish at salamanca, while the enemy's guns were pouring shot into his regiment, sir william napier's men became disobedient. he at once ordered a halt, and flogged four of the ringleaders under fire. the men yielded at once, and then marched three miles under a heavy cannonade as coolly as if it were a review.

execute your resolutions immediately. thoughts are but dreams till their effects be tried. does competition trouble you? work away; what is your competitor but a man? *conquer your place in the world*, for all things serve a brave soul. combat difficulty manfully; sustain misfortune bravely; endure poverty nobly; encounter disappointment courageously. the influence of the brave man is a magnetism which creates an epidemic of noble zeal in all about him. every day sends to the grave obscure men, who have only remained in obscurity because their timidity has prevented them from making a first effort; and who, if they could have been induced to begin, would, in all probability, have gone great lengths in the career of usefulness and fame. "no great deed is done," says george eliot, "by falterers who ask for certainty." the brave, cheerful man will survive his blighted hopes and disappointments, take them for just what they are, lessons and perhaps blessings in disguise, and will march boldly and cheerfully forward in the battle of life. or, if necessary, he will bear his ills with a patience and calm endurance deeper than ever plummet sounded. he is the true hero.

then to side with truth is noble when we share her wretched crust,
ere her cause bring fame and profit, and 't is prosperous to be just;
then it is the brave man chooses, while the coward stands aside,
doubting in his abject spirit, till his lord is crucified.
lowell.

our doubts are traitors,
and make us lose the good we oft might win,
by fearing to attempt.
shakespeare.

after the great inward struggle was over, and he had determined to remain loyal to his principles, thomas more walked cheerfully to the block. his wife called him a fool for staying in a dark, damp, filthy prison when he might have his liberty by merely renouncing his doctrines, as some of the bishops had done. but he preferred death to dishonor. his daughter allowed the power of love to drive away fear. she remained true to her father when all others, even her mother, had forsaken him. after his head had been cut off and exhibited on a pole on london bridge, the poor girl begged it of the authorities, and requested that it be buried in the coffin with her. her request was granted, for her death occurred soon.

when sir walter raleigh came to the scaffold he was very faint, and began his speech to the crowd by saying that during the last two days he had been visited by two ague fits. "if, therefore, you perceive any weakness in me, i beseech you ascribe it to my sickness rather than to myself." he took the axe and kissed the blade, and said to the sheriff: "'t is a sharp medicine, but a sound cure for all diseases."

don't waste time dreaming of obstacles you may never encounter, or in crossing bridges you have not reached. don't fool with a nettle! grasp with firmness if you would rob it of its sting. to half will and to hang forever in the balance is to lose your grip on life.

abraham lincoln's boyhood was one long struggle with poverty, with little education, and no influential friends. when at last he had begun the practice of law, it required no little daring to cast his fortune with the weaker side in politics, and thus imperil what small reputation he had gained. only the most sublime moral courage could have sustained him as president to hold his ground against hostile criticism and a long train of disaster; to issue the emancipation proclamation; to support grant and stanton against the clamor of the politicians and the press; and through it all to do the right as god gave him to see the right.

lincoln never shrank from espousing an unpopular cause when he believed it to be right. at the time when it almost cost a young lawyer his bread and butter to defend the fugitive slave, and when other lawyers had refused, lincoln would always plead the cause of the unfortunate whenever an opportunity presented. "go to lincoln," people would say, when these hounded fugitives were seeking protection; "he's not afraid of any cause, if it's right."

as salmon p. chase left the court room after making an impassioned plea for the runaway slave girl matilda, a man looked at him in surprise and said: "there goes a fine young fellow who has just ruined himself." but in thus ruining himself chase had taken the first important step in a career in which he became governor of ohio, united states senator from ohio, secretary of the united states treasury, and chief justice of the united states supreme court.

at the trial of william penn for having spoken at a quaker meeting, the recorder, not satisfied with the first verdict, said to the jury: "we will have a verdict by the help of god, or you shall starve for it." "you are englishmen," said penn; "mind your privileges, give not away your right." at last the jury, after two days and two nights without food, returned a verdict of "not guilty." the recorder fined them forty marks apiece for their independence.

what cared christ for the jeers of the crowd? the palsied hand moved, the blind saw, the leper was made whole, the dead spake, despite the ridicule and scoffs of the spectators.

what cared wendell phillips for rotten eggs, derisive scorn, and hisses? in him "at last the scornful world had met its match." were beecher and gough to be silenced by the rude english mobs that came to extinguish them? no! they held their ground and compelled unwilling thousands to hear and to heed. did anna dickinson leave the platform when the pistol bullets of the molly maguires flew about her head? she silenced those pistols by her courage and her arguments.

"what the world wants is a knox, who dares to preach on with a musket leveled at his head, a garrison, who is not afraid of a jail, or a mob, or a scaffold erected in front of his door.

"storms may howl around thee,
foes may hunt and hound thee:
shall they overpower thee?
never, never, never."

when general butler was sent with nine thousand men to quell the new york riots, he arrived in advance of his troops, and found the streets thronged with an angry mob, which had already hanged more than one man to lamp-posts. without waiting for his men, butler went to the place where the crowd was most dense, overturned an ash barrel, stood upon it, and began: "delegates from five points, fiends from hell, you have murdered your superiors," and the blood-stained crowd quailed before the courageous words of a single man in a city which mayor fernando wood could not restrain with the aid of police and militia.

"our enemies are before us," exclaimed the spartans at thermopylae. "and we are before them," was the cool reply of leonidas. "deliver your arms," came the message from xerxes. "come and take them," was the answer leonidas sent back. a persian soldier said: "you will not be able to see the sun for flying javelins and arrows." "then we will fight in the shade," replied a lacedemonian. what wonder that a handful of such men checked the march of the greatest host that ever trod the earth.

"it is impossible," said a staff officer, when napoleon gave directions for a daring plan. "impossible!" thundered the great commander, "*impossible* is the adjective of fools!" napoleon went to the edge of his possibility.

grant never knew when he was beaten. when told that he was surrounded by the enemy at belmont, he quietly replied: "well, then we must cut our way out."

the courageous man is an example to the intrepid. his influence is magnetic. he creates an epidemic of nobleness. men follow him, even to the death.

the spirit of courage will transform the whole temper of your life. "the wise and active conquer difficulties by daring to attempt them. sloth and folly shiver and sicken at the sight of trial and hazard, and make the impossibility they fear."

"the hero," says emerson, "is the man who is immovably centred."

emin pasha, the explorer of africa, was left behind by his exploring party under circumstances that were thought certainly fatal, and his death was reported with great assurance. early the next winter, as his troop was on its toilsome but exciting way through central africa, it came upon a most wretched sight. a party of natives had been kidnapped by the slave-hunters, and dragged in chains thus far toward the land of bondage. but small-pox had set in, and the miserable company had been abandoned to their fate. emin sent his men ahead, and stayed behind in this camp of death to act as physician and nurse. how many lives he saved is not known, though it is known that he nearly lost his own. the age of chivalry is not gone by. this is as knightly a deed as poet ever chronicled.

a mouse that dwelt near the abode of a great magician was kept in such constant distress by its fear of a cat, that the magician, taking pity on it, turned it into a cat itself. immediately it began to suffer from its fear of a dog, so the magician turned it into a dog. then it began to suffer from fear of a tiger. the magician therefore turned it into a tiger. then it began to suffer from fear of hunters, and the magician said in disgust: "be a mouse again. as you have only the heart of a mouse, it is impossible to help you by giving you the body of a nobler animal."

men who have dared have moved the world, often before reaching the prime of life. it is astonishing what daring to begin and perseverance have enabled even youths to achieve. alexander, who ascended the throne at twenty, had conquered the known world before dying at thirty-three. julius caesar captured eight hundred cities, conquered three hundred nations, and defeated three million men, became a great orator and one of the greatest statesmen known, and still was a young man. washington was appointed adjutant-general at nineteen, was sent at twenty-one as an ambassador to treat with the french, and won his first battle as a colonel at twenty-two. lafayette was made general of the whole french army at twenty. charlemagne was master of france and germany at thirty. conde was only twenty-two when he conquered at rocroi. galileo was but eighteen when he saw the principle of the pendulum in the swinging lamp in the cathedral at pisa. peel was in parliament at twenty-one. gladstone was in parliament before he was twenty-two, and at twenty-four he was lord of the treasury. elizabeth barrett browning was proficient in greek and latin at twelve; de quincey at eleven. robert browning wrote at eleven poetry of no mean order. cowley, who sleeps in westminster abbey, published a volume of poems at fifteen. n. p. willis won lasting fame as a poet before leaving college. macaulay was a celebrated author before he was twenty-three. luther was but twenty-nine when he nailed his famous thesis to the door of the bishop and defied the pope. nelson was a lieutenant in the british navy before he was twenty. he was but forty-seven when he received his death wound at trafalgar. charles the twelfth was only nineteen when he gained the battle of narva; at thirty-six, cortez was the conqueror of mexico; at thirty-two, clive had established the british power in india. hannibal, the greatest of military commanders, was only thirty when, at cannae, he dealt an almost annihilating blow at the republic of rome; and napoleon was only twenty-seven when, on the plains of italy, he outgeneraled and defeated, one after another, the veteran marshals of austria.

equal courage and resolution are often shown by men who have passed the allotted limit of life. victor hugo and wellington were both in their prime after they had reached the age of threescore years and ten. george bancroft wrote some of his best historical work when he was eighty-five. gladstone ruled england with a strong hand at eighty-four, and was a marvel of literary and scholarly ability.

"not every vessel that sails from tarshish will bring back the gold of ophir. but shall it therefore rot in the harbor? no! give its sails to the wind!"

shakespeare says: "he is not worthy of the honeycomb that shuns the hive because the bees have stings."

"the brave man is not he who feels no fear,
for that were stupid and irrational;
but he whose noble soul its fear subdues
and bravely dares the danger nature shrinks from."

the inscription on the gates of busyrane: "be bold." on the second gate: "be bold, be bold, and ever more be bold;" the third gate: "be not too bold."

many a bright youth has accomplished nothing of worth simply because he did not dare to commence.

begin! begin!! begin!!!

whatever people may think of you, do that which you believe to be right. be alike indifferent to censure or praise.--pythagoras.

fear makes man a slave to others. this is the tyrant's chain. anxiety is a form of cowardice embittering life.--channing.

courage is generosity of the highest order, for the brave are prodigal of the most precious things. our blood is nearer and dearer to us than our money, and our life than our estate. women are more taken with courage than with generosity.--colton.

who chooses me must give and hazard all he hath.
*merchant of venice*, inscription on leaden casket.

i dare to do all that may become a man:
who dares do more is none.
shakespeake.

for man's great actions are performed in minor struggles. there are obstinate and unknown braves who defend themselves inch by inch in the shadows against the fatal invasion of want and turpitude. there are noble and mysterious triumphs which no eye sees, no renown rewards, and no flourish of trumpets salutes. life, misfortune, isolation, abandonment, and poverty are battlefields which have their heroes.--victor hugo.

who waits until the wind shall silent keep,
who never finds the ready hour to sow,
who watcheth clouds, will have no time to reap.
helen hunt jackson.

quit yourselves like men.--1 samuel iv. 9.

# CHAPTER III.

## the will and the way.

"the 'way' will be found by a resolute will."

"i will find a way or make one."

nothing is impossible to the man who can will.--mirabeau.

a politician weakly and amiably in the right is no match for a politician tenaciously and pugnaciously in the wrong.--e. p. whipple.

the iron will of one stout heart shall make a thousand quail;
a feeble dwarf, dauntlessly resolved, will turn the tide of battle,
and rally to a nobler strife the giants that had fled.
tupper.

"man alone can perform the impossible. they can who think they can. character is a perfectly educated will."

the education of the will is the object of our existence. for the resolute and determined there is time and opportunity.--emerson.

invincible determination, and a right nature, are the levers that move the world.--president porter.

in the lexicon of youth which fate reserves for a bright manhood there is no such word as fail.--bulwer.

perpetual pushing and assurance put a difficulty out of countenance and make a seeming difficulty give way.--jeremy collier.

when a firm and decisive spirit is recognized, it is curious to see how the space clears around a man and leaves him room and freedom.--john foster.

the star of the unconquered will,
he rises in my breast,
serene, and resolute and still,
and calm and self-possessed.

longfellow.

"as well can the prince of orange pluck the stars from the sky, as bring the ocean to the wall of leyden for your relief," was the derisive shout of the spanish soldiers when told that the dutch fleet would raise that terrible four months' siege of 1574. but from the parched lips of william, tossing on his bed of fever at rotterdam, had issued the command: "*break down the dikes: give holland back to ocean:*" and the people had replied: "better a drowned land than a lost land." they began to demolish dike after dike of the strong lines, ranged one within another for fifteen miles to their city of the interior. it was an enormous task; the garrison was starving; and the besiegers laughed in scorn at the slow progress of the puny insects who sought to rule the waves of the sea. but ever, as of old, heaven aids those who help themselves. on the first and second of october a violent equinoctial gale rolled the ocean inland, and swept the fleet on the rising waters almost to the camp of the spaniards. the next morning the garrison sallied out to attack their enemies, but the besiegers had fled in terror under cover of the darkness. the next day the wind changed, and a counter tempest brushed the water, with the fleet upon it, from the surface of holland. the outer dikes were replaced at once, leaving the north sea within its old bounds. when the flowers bloomed the following spring, a joyous procession marched through the streets to found the university of leyden, in commemoration of the wonderful deliverance of the city.

* * * * * *

"the wizard of the north."

"so nigh is grandeur to our dust,
so near is god to man,
when duty whispers low, 'thou must,'
the youth replies, 'i can.'"

* * * * * *

at a dinner party given in 1837, at the residence of chancellor kent, in new york city, some of the most distinguished men in the country were invited, and among them was a young and rather melancholy and reticent frenchman. professor morse was one of the guests, and during the evening he drew the attention of mr. gallatin, then a prominent statesman, to the stranger, observing that his forehead indicated great intellect. "yes," replied mr. gallatin, touching his own forehead with his finger, "there is a great deal in that head of his: but he has a strange fancy. can you believe it? he has the idea that he will one day be the emperor of france. can you conceive anything more absurd?"

it did seem absurd, for this reserved frenchman was then a poor adventurer, an exile from his country, without fortune or powerful connections, and yet, fourteen years later, his idea became a fact,--his dream of becoming napoleon iii. was realized. true, before he accomplished his purpose there were long dreary years of imprisonment, exile, disaster, and patient labor and hope, but he gained his ambition at last. he was not scrupulous as to the means employed to accomplish his ends, yet he is a remarkable example of what pluck and energy can do.

when it was proposed to unite england and america by steam, dr. lardner delivered a lecture before the royal society "proving" that steamers could never cross the atlantic, because they could not carry coal enough to produce steam during the whole voyage. the passage of the steamship sirius, which crossed in nineteen days, was fatal to lardner's theory. when it was proposed to build a vessel of iron, many persons said: "iron sinks--only wood can float:" but experiments proved that the miracle of the prophet in making iron "swim" could be repeated, and now not only ships of war, but merchant vessels, are built of iron or steel. a will found a way to make iron float.

mr. ingram, publisher of the "london illustrated news," who lost his life on lake michigan, walked ten miles to deliver a single paper rather than disappoint a customer, when he began life as a newsdealer at nottingham, england. does any one wonder that such a youth succeeded? once he rose at two o'clock in the morning and walked to london to get some papers because there was no post to bring them. he determined that his customers should not be disappointed. this is the kind of will that finds a way.

there is scarcely anything in all biography grander than the saying of young henry fawcett, gladstone's last postmaster-general, to his grief-stricken father, who had put out both his eyes by bird-shot during a game hunt: "never mind, father, blindness shall not interfere with my success in life." one of the most pathetic sights in london streets, long afterward, was henry fawcett, m. p., led everywhere by a faithful daughter, who acted as amanuensis as well as guide to her plucky father. think of a young man, scarcely on the threshold of active life, suddenly losing the sight of both eyes and yet, by mere pluck and almost incomprehensible tenacity of purpose, lifting himself into eminence, in any direction, to say nothing of becoming one of the foremost men in a country noted for its great men. most youth would have succumbed to such a misfortune, and would never have been heard from again. but fortunately for the world, there are yet left many fawcetts, many prescotts, parkmans, cavanaghs.

the courageous daughter who was eyes to her father was herself a marvelous example of pluck and determination. for the first time in the history of oxford college, which reaches back centuries, she succeeded in winning the post which had only been gained before by great men, such as gladstone,--the post of senior wrangler. this achievement had had no parallel in history up to that date, and attracted the attention of the whole civilized world. not only had no woman ever held this position before, but with few exceptions it had only been held by men who in after life became highly distinguished. who can deny that where there is a will, as a rule, there's a way?

when grant was a boy he could not find "can't" in the dictionary. it is the men who have no "can't" in their dictionaries that make things move.

"circumstances," says milton, "have rarely favored famous men. they have fought their way to triumph through all sorts of opposing obstacles."

the true way to conquer circumstances is to be a greater circumstance yourself.

yet, while desiring to impress in the most forcible manner possible the fact that will-power is necessary to success, and that, other things being equal, the greater the will-power, the grander and more complete the success, we cannot indorse the preposterous theory that there is nothing in circumstances or environments, or that any man, simply because he has an indomitable will, may become a bonaparte, a pitt, a webster, a beecher, a lincoln. we must temper determination with discretion, and support it with knowledge and common sense, or it will only lead us to run our heads against posts. we must not expect to overcome a stubborn fact by a stubborn will. we merely have the right to assume that we can do anything within the limit of our utmost faculty, strength, and endurance. obstacles permanently insurmountable bar our progress in some directions, but in any direction we may reasonably hope and attempt to go, we shall find that the obstacles, as a rule, are either not insurmountable or else not permanent. the strong-willed, intelligent, persistent man will find or make a way where, in the nature of things, a way can be found or made.

every schoolboy knows that circumstances do give clients to lawyers and patients to physicians; place ordinary clergymen in extraordinary pulpits; place sons of the rich at the head of immense corporations and large houses, when they have very ordinary ability and scarcely any experience, while poor young men with extraordinary abilities, good education, good character, and large experience, often have to fight their way for years to obtain even very ordinary situations. every one knows that there are thousands of young men, both in the city and in the country, of superior ability, who seem to be compelled by circumstances to remain in very ordinary positions for small pay, when others about them are raised by money or family influence into desirable places. in other words, we all know that the best men do not always get the best places: circumstances do have a great deal to do with our position, our salaries, and our station in life.

many young men who are nature's noblemen, who are natural leaders, are working under superintendents, foremen, and managers infinitely their inferiors, but whom circumstances have placed above them and will keep there, unless some emergency makes merit indispensable. no, the race is not always to the swift.

every one knows that there is not always a way where there is a will, that labor does not always conquer all things; that there are things impossible even to him that wills, however strongly; that one cannot always make anything of himself he chooses; that there are limitations in our very natures which no amount of will-power or industry can overcome; that no amount of sun-staring can ever make an eagle out of a crow.

the simple truth is that a will strong enough to keep a man continually striving for things not wholly beyond his powers will carry him in time very far toward his chosen goal.

the greatest thing a man can do in this world is to make the most possible out of the stuff that has been given to him. this is success, and there is no other.

while it is true that our circumstances or environments do affect us, in most things they do not prevent our growth. the corn that is now ripe, whence comes it, and what is it? is it not large or small, stunted wild maize or well-developed ears, according to the conditions under which it has grown? yet its environments cannot make wheat of it. nor can our circumstances alter our nature. it is part of our nature, and wholly within our power, greatly to change and to take advantage of our circumstances, so that, unlike the corn, we can rise much superior to our natural surroundings simply because we can thus vary and improve the surroundings. in other words, man can usually build the very road on which he is to run his race.

it is not a question of what some one else can do or become, which every youth should ask himself, but what can i do? how can i develop myself into the grandest possible manhood?

so far, then, from the power of circumstances being a hindrance to men in trying to build for themselves an imperial highway to fortune, these circumstances constitute the very quarry out of which they are to get paving-stones for the road.

while it is true that the will-power cannot perform miracles, yet that it is almost omnipotent, that it can perform wonders, all history goes to prove. as shakespeare says:--

"men at some time are masters of their fates:
the fault, dear brutus, is not in our stars,
but in ourselves, that we are underlings."

"there is nobody," says a roman cardinal, "whom fortune does not visit once in his life: but when she finds he is not ready to receive her, she goes in at the door, and out through the window." opportunity is coy. the carcless, the slow, the unobservant, the lazy fail to see it, or clutch at it when it has gone. the sharp fellows detect it instantly, and catch it when on the wing.

show me a man who is, according to popular prejudice, a victim of bad luck, and i will show you one who has some unfortunate crooked twist of temperament that invites disaster. he is ill-tempered, or conceited, or trifling; lacks character, enthusiasm, or some other requisite for success.

disraeli says that man is not the creature of circumstances, but that circumstances are the creatures of men.

what has chance ever done in the world? has it built any cities? has it invented any telephones, any telegraphs? has it built any steamships, established any universities, any asylums, any hospitals? was there any chance in caesar's crossing the rubicon? what had chance to do with napoleon's career, with wellington's, or grant's, or von moltke's? every battle was won before it was begun. what had luck to do with thermopylae, trafalgar, gettysburg? our successes we ascribe to ourselves; our failures to destiny.

man is not a helpless atom in this vast creation, with a fixed position, and naught to do but obey his own polarity.

believe in the power of will, which annihilates the sickly, sentimental doctrine of fatalism,--you must but can't, you ought but it is impossible.

give me the man

"who breaks his birth's invidious bar,
and grasps the skirts of happy chance,
and breasts the blows of circumstance,
and grapples with his evil star."

it is only the ignorant and superficial who believe in fate. "the first step into thought lifts this mountain of necessity." "fate is unpenetrated causes." "they may well fear fate who have any infirmity of habit or aim: but he who rests on what he is has a destiny beyond destiny, and can make mouths at fortune."

the indomitable will, the inflexible purpose, will find a way or make one. there is always room for a man of force.

"he who has a firm will," says goethe, "moulds the world to himself." "people do not lack strength," says victor hugo, "they lack will."

"he who resolves upon any great end, by that very resolution has scaled the great barriers to it, and he who seizes the grand idea of self-cultivation, and solemnly resolves upon it, will find that idea, that resolution, burning like fire within him, and ever putting him upon his own improvement. he will find it removing difficulties, searching out, or making means; giving courage for despondency, and strength for weakness."

nearly all great men, those who have towered high above their fellows, have been remarkable above all things else for their energy of will. of julius caesar it was said by a contemporary that it was his activity and giant determination, rather than his military skill, that won his victories. the youth who starts out in life determined to make the most of his eyes and let nothing escape him which he can possibly use for his own advancement; who keeps his ears open for every sound that can help him on his way, who keeps his hands open that he may clutch every opportunity, who is ever on the alert for everything which can help him to get on in the world, who seizes every experience in life and grinds it up into paint for his great life's picture, who keeps his heart open that he may catch every noble impulse, and everything which may inspire him,--that youth will be sure to make his life successful; there are no "ifs" or "ands" about it. if he has his health, nothing can keep him from final success.

no tyranny of circumstances can permanently imprison a determined will.

the world always stands aside for the determined man. will makes a way, even through seeming impossibilities. "it is the half a neck nearer that shows the blood and wins the race; the one march more that wins the campaign: the five minutes more of unyielding courage that wins the fight." again and again had the irrepressible carter harrison been consigned to oblivion by the educated and moral element of chicago. nothing could keep him down. he was invincible. a son of chicago, he had partaken of that nineteenth century miracle, that phoenix-like nature of the city which, though she was burned, caused her to rise from her ashes and become a greater and a grander chicago, a wonder of the world. carter harrison would not down. he entered the democratic convention and, with an audacity rarely equaled, in spite of their protest, boldly declared himself their candidate. every newspaper in chicago, save the "times," his own paper, bitterly opposed his election: but notwithstanding all opposition, he was elected by twenty thousand majority. the aristocrats hated him, the moral element feared him, but the poor people believed in him: he pandered to them, flattered them, till they elected him. while we would not by any means hold carter harrison up to youth as a model, yet there is a great lesson in his will-power and wonderful tenacity of purpose.

"the general of a large army may be defeated," said confucius, "but you cannot defeat the determined mind of a peasant."

the poor, deaf pauper, kitto, who made shoes in the almshouse, and who became the greatest of biblical scholars, wrote in his journal, on the threshold of manhood: "i am not myself a believer in impossibilities: i think that all the fine stories about natural ability, etc., are mere rigmarole, and that every man may, according to his opportunities and industry, render himself almost anything he wishes to become."

years ago, a young mechanic took a bath in the river clyde. while swimming from shore to shore he discerned a beautiful bank, uncultivated, and he then and there resolved to be the owner of it, and to adorn it, and to build upon it the finest mansion in all the borough, and name it in honor of the maiden to whom he was espoused. "last summer," says a well-known american, "i had the pleasure of dining in that princely mansion, and receiving this fact from the lips of the great shipbuilder of the clyde." that one purpose was made the ruling passion of his life, and all the energies of his soul were put in requisition for its accomplishment.

lincoln is probably the most remarkable example on the pages of history, showing the possibilities of our country. from the poverty in which he was born, through the rowdyism of a frontier town, the rudeness of frontier society, the discouragement of early bankruptcy, and the fluctuations of popular politics, he rose to the championship of union and freedom.

lincoln's will made his way. when his friends nominated him as a candidate for the legislature, his enemies made fun of him. when making his campaign speeches he wore a mixed jean coat so short that he could not sit down on it, flax and tow-linen trousers, straw hat, and pot-metal boots. he had nothing in the world but character and friends.

when his friends suggested law to him, he laughed at the idea of his being a lawyer. he said he hadn't brains enough. he read law barefoot under the trees, his neighbors said, and he sometimes slept on the counter in the store where he worked. he had to borrow money to buy a suit of clothes to make a respectable appearance in the legislature, and walked to take his seat at vandalia,--one hundred miles. while he was in the legislature, john f. stuart, an eminent lawyer of springfield, told him how clay had even inferior chances to his, had got all of the education he had in a log schoolhouse without windows or doors; and finally induced lincoln to study law.

see thurlow weed, defying poverty and wading through the snow two miles, with rags for shoes, to borrow a book to read before the sap-bush fire. see locke, living on bread and water in a dutch garret. see heyne, sleeping many a night on a barn floor with only a book for his pillow. see samuel drew, tightening his apron strings "in lieu of a dinner." see young lord eldon, before daylight copying coke on littleton over and over again. history is full of such examples. he who will pay the price for victory needs never fear final defeat. why were the roman legionaries victorious?

"for romans, in rome's quarrels,
spared neither land nor gold,
nor son, nor wife, nor limb nor life,
in the brave days of old."

fowell buxton, writing to one of his sons, says: "i am sure that a young man may be very much what he pleases."

dr. mathews has well said that "there is hardly a word in the whole human vocabulary which is more cruelly abused than the word 'luck.' to all the faults and failures of men, their positive sins and their less culpable shortcomings, it is made to stand a godfather and sponsor. go talk with the bankrupt man of business, who has swamped his fortune by wild speculation, extravagance of living, or lack of energy, and you will find that he vindicates his wonderful self-love by confounding the steps which he took indiscreetly with those to which he was forced by 'circumstances,' and complacently regarding himself as the victim of ill-luck. go visit the incarcerated criminal, who has imbued his hands in the blood of his fellow-man, or who is guilty of less heinous crimes, and you will find that, joining the temptations which were easy to avoid with those which were comparatively irresistible, he has hurriedly patched up a treaty with conscience, and stifles its compunctious visitings by persuading himself that, from first to last, he was the victim of circumstances. go talk with the mediocre in talents and attainments, the weak-spirited man who, from lack of energy and application, has made but little headway in the world, being outstripped in the race of life by those whom he had despised as his inferiors, and you will find that he, too, acknowledges the all-potent power of luck, and soothes his humbled pride by deeming himself the victim of ill-fortune. in short, from the most venial offense to the most flagrant, there is hardly any wrong act or neglect to which this too fatally convenient word is not applied as a palliation."

paris was in the hands of a mob, the authorities were panic-stricken, for they did not dare to trust their underlings. in came a man who said, "i know a young officer who has the courage and ability to quell this mob." "send for him; send for him; send for him," said they. napoleon was sent for, came, subjugated the mob, subjugated the authorities, ruled france, then conquered europe.

what a lesson is napoleon's life for the sickly, wishy-washy, dwarfed, sentimental "dudes," hanging about our cities, country, and universities, complaining of their hard lot, dreaming of success, and wondering why they are left in the rear in the great race of life.

success in life is dependent largely upon the willpower, and whatever weakens or impairs it diminishes success. the will can be educated. that which most easily becomes a habit in us is the will. learn, then, to will decisively and strongly; thus fix your floating life, and leave it no longer to be carried hither and thither, like a withered leaf, by every wind that blows. "it is not talent that men lack, it is the will to labor; it is the purpose, not the power to produce."

it was this insatiable thirst for knowledge which held to his task, through poverty and discouragement, john leyden, a scotch shepherd's son. barefoot and alone, he walked six or eight miles daily to learn to read, which was all the schooling he had. his desire for an education defied the extremest poverty, and no obstacle could turn him from his purpose. he was rich when he discovered a little bookstore, and his thirsty soul would drink in the precious treasures from its priceless volumes for hours, perfectly oblivious of the scanty meal of bread and water which awaited him at his lowly lodging. nothing could discourage him from trying to improve himself by study. it seemed to him that an opportunity to get at books and lectures was all that any man could need. before he was nineteen, this poor shepherd boy with no chance had astonished the professors of edinburgh by his knowledge of greek and latin.

hearing that a surgeon's assistant in the civil service was wanted, although he knew nothing whatever of medicine, he determined to apply for it. there were only six months before the place was to be filled, but nothing could daunt him, and in six months' time he actually took his degree with honor. walter scott, who thought this one of the most remarkable illustrations of perseverance, helped to fit him out, and he sailed for india.

webster was very poor even after he entered dartmouth college. a friend sent him a recipe for greasing his boots. webster wrote and thanked him, and added: "but my boots need other doctoring, for they not only admit water, but even peas and gravel-stones." yet he became one of the greatest men in the world. sydney smith said: "webster was a living lie, because no man on earth could be as great as he looked." carlyle said of him: "one would incline at sight to back him against the world."

what seemed to be luck followed stephen girard all his life. no matter what he did, it always seemed to others to turn to his account. his coming to philadelphia seemed a lucky accident. a sloop was seen one morning off the mouth of delaware bay floating the flag of france and a signal of distress. young girard was captain of this sloop, and was on his way to a canadian port with freight from new orleans. an american skipper, seeing his distress, went to his aid, but told him the american war had broken out, and that the british cruisers were all along the american coast, and would seize his vessel. he told him his only chance was to make a push for philadelphia. girard did not know the way, and had no money. the skipper loaned him five dollars to get the service of a pilot who demanded his money in advance.

his sloop passed into the delaware just in time to avoid capture by a british war vessel. he sold the sloop and cargo in philadelphia, and began business on the capital. being a foreigner, unable to speak english, short, stout, and with a repulsive face, blind in one eye, it was hard for him to get a start. but he was not the man to give up. he had begun as a cabin boy at thirteen, and for nine years sailed between bordeaux and the french west indies. he improved every leisure minute at sea, mastering the art of navigation.

at the age of eight he first discovered that he was blind in one eye. his father, evidently thinking that he would never amount to anything, would not help him to an education beyond that of mere reading and writing, but sent his younger brothers to college. the discovery of his blindness, the neglect of his father, and the chagrin of his brothers' advancement, soured his whole life.

when he began business for himself in philadelphia, there seemed to be nothing he would not do for money. he bought and sold anything, from groceries to old junk. he bottled wine and cider, from which he made a good profit. everything he touched prospered. in 1780, he resumed the new orleans and st. domingo trade, in which he had been engaged at the breaking out of the revolution. here great success again attended him. he had two vessels lying in one of the st. domingo ports when the great insurrection on that island broke out. a number of the rich planters fled to his vessels with their valuables, which they left for safe keeping while they went back to their estates to secure more. they probably fell victims to the cruel negroes, for they never returned, and girard was the lucky possessor of $50,000 which the goods brought in philadephia.

everybody, especially his jealous brother merchants, attributed his great success to his luck. while undoubtedly he was fortunate in happening to be at the right place at the right time, yet he was precision, method, accuracy, energy itself. he left nothing to chance. his plans and schemes were worked out with mathematical care. his letters, written to his captains in foreign ports, laying out their routes and giving detailed instruction from which they were never allowed to deviate under any circumstances, are models of foresight and systematic planning. he never left anything of importance to others. he was rigidly accurate in his instructions, and would not allow the slightest departure from them. he used to say that while his captains might save him money by deviating from instructions once, yet they would cause loss in ninety-nine other cases. once, when a captain returned and had saved him several thousand dollars by buying his cargo of cheese in another port than that in which he had been instructed to buy, girard was so enraged, although he was several thousand dollars richer, that he discharged the captain on the spot, notwithstanding the latter had been faithful in his service for many years, and thought he was saving his employer a great deal of money by deviating from his instructions.

girard lived in a dingy little house, poorer than that occupied by many of his employees. he married a servant girl of great beauty, but she proved totally unfitted for him, and died at last in the insane asylum.

girard never lost a ship, and many times what brought financial ruin to many others, as the war of 1812, only increased his wealth. what seemed luck with him was only good judgment and promptness in seizing opportunities, and the greatest care and zeal in improving them to their utmost possibilities.

luck is not god's price for success: that is altogether too cheap, nor does he dicker with men.

the mathematician tells you that if you throw the dice, there are thirty chances to one against your turning up a particular number, and a hundred to one against your repeating the same throw three times in succession: and so on in an augmenting ratio. what is luck? is it, as has been suggested, a blind man's buff among the laws? a ruse among the elements? a trick of dame nature? has any scholar defined luck? any philosopher explained its nature? any chemist shown its composition? is luck that strange, nondescript fairy, that does all things among men that they cannot account for? if so, why does not luck make a fool speak words of wisdom; an ignoramus utter lectures on philosophy?

many a young man who has read the story of john wanamaker's romantic career has gained very little inspiration or help from it toward his own elevation and advancement, for he looks upon it as the result of good luck, chance, or fate. "what a lucky fellow," he says to himself as he reads; "what a bonanza he fell into." but a careful analysis of wanamaker's life only enforces the same lesson taught by the analysis of most great lives, namely, that a good mother, a good constitution, the habit of hard work, indomitable energy, a determination which knows no defeat, a decision which never wavers, a concentration which never scatters its forces, courage which never falters, a self-mastery which can say no, and stick to it, an "ignominious love of detail," strict integrity and downright honesty, a cheerful disposition, unbounded enthusiasm in one's calling, and a high aim and noble purpose insure a very large measure of success.

youth should be taught that there is something in circumstances; that there is such a thing as a poor pedestrian happening to find no obstruction in his way, and reaching the goal when a better walker finds the drawbridge up, the street blockaded, and so fails to win the race; that wealth often does place unworthy sons in high positions, that family influence does gain a lawyer clients, a physician patients, an ordinary scholar a good professorship; but that, on the other hand, position, clients, patients, professorships, manager's and superintendent's positions do not necessarily constitute success. he should be taught that in the long run, as a rule, *the best man does win the best place*, and that persistent merit does succeed.

there is about as much chance of idleness and incapacity winning real success, or a high position in life, as there would be in producing a paradise lost by shaking up promiscuously the separate words of webster's dictionary, and letting them fall at random on the floor. fortune smiles upon those who roll up their sleeves and put their shoulders to the wheel; upon men who are not afraid of dreary, dry, irksome drudgery, men of nerve and grit who do not turn aside for dirt and detail.

the youth should be taught that "he alone is great, who, by a life heroic, conquers fate;" that "diligence is the mother of good luck;" that, nine times out of ten, what we call luck or fate is but a mere bugbear of the indolent, the languid, the purposeless, the careless, the indifferent; that the man who fails, as a rule, does not see or seize his opportunity. opportunity is coy, is swift, is gone, before the slow, the unobservant, the indolent, or the careless can seize her:--

"in idle wishes fools supinely stay:
be there a will and wisdom finds a way."

it has been well said that the very reputation of being strong willed, plucky, and indefatigable is of priceless value. it often cows enemies and dispels at the start opposition to one's undertakings which would otherwise be formidable.

"if eric's in robust health, and has slept well, and is at the top of his condition, and thirty years old at his departure from greenland," says emerson, "he will steer west and his ships will reach newfoundland. but take eric out and put in a stronger and bolder man, and the ships will sail six hundred, one thousand, fifteen hundred miles further, and reach labrador and new england. there is no chance in results." obstacles tower before the living man like mountain chains, stopping his path and hindering his progress. he surmounts them by his energy. he makes a new path over them. he climbs upon them to mountain heights. they cannot stop him. they do not much delay him. he transmutes difficulties into power, and makes temporary failures into stepping-stones to ultimate success.

how many might have been giants who are only dwarfs. how many a one has died "with all his music in him."

it is astonishing what men who have come to their senses late in life have accomplished by a sudden resolution.

arkwright was fifty years of age when he began to learn english grammar and improve his writing and spelling. benjamin franklin was past fifty before he began the study of science and philosophy. milton, in his blindness, was past the age of fifty when he sat down to complete his world-known epic, and scott at fifty-five took up his pen to redeem an enormous liability. "yet i am learning," said michael angelo, when threescore years and ten were past, and he had long attained the highest triumphs of his art.

even brains are second in importance to will. the vacillating man is always pushed aside in the race of life. it is only the weak and vacillating who halt before adverse circumstances and obstacles. a man with an iron will, with a determination that nothing shall check his career, if he has perseverance and grit, is sure to succeed. we may not find time for what we would like, but what we long for and strive for with all our strength, we usually approximate if we do not fully reach. hunger breaks through stone walls; stern necessity will find a way or make one.

success is also a great physical as well as mental tonic, and tends to strengthen the will-power. dr. johnson says: "resolutions and success reciprocally produce each other." strong-willed men, as a rule, are successful men, and great success is almost impossible without it.

a man who can resolve vigorously upon a course of action, and turns neither to the right nor the left, though a paradise tempt him, who keeps his eyes upon the goal, whatever distracts him, is sure of success. we could almost classify successes and failures by their various degrees of will-power. men like sir james mackintosh, coleridge, la harpe, and many others who have dazzled the world with their brilliancy, but who never accomplished a tithe of what they attempted, who were always raising our expectations that they were about to perform wonderful deeds, but who accomplished nothing worthy of their abilities, have been deficient in will-power. one talent with a will behind it will accomplish more than ten without it. the great linguist of bologna mastered a hundred languages by taking them singly, as the lion fought the bulls.

i wish it were possible to show the youth of america the great part that the will might play in their success in life and in their happiness also. the achievements of will-power are simply beyond computation. scarcely anything in reason seems impossible to the man who can will strong enough and long enough.

how often we see this illustrated in the case of a young woman who suddenly becomes conscious that she is plain and unattractive; who, by prodigious exercise of her will and untiring industry, resolves to redeem herself from obscurity and commonness; and who not only makes up for her deficiencies, but elevates herself into a prominence and importance which mere personal attractions could never have given her. charlotte cushman, without a charm of form or face, climbed to the very top of her profession. how many young men, stung by consciousness of physical deformity or mental deficiencies, have, by a strong persistent exercise of will-power, raised themselves from mediocrity and placed themselves high above those who scorned them.

history is full of examples of men and women who have redeemed themselves from disgrace, poverty, and misfortune, by the firm resolution of an iron will. the consciousness of being looked upon as inferior, as incapable of accomplishing what others accomplish; the sensitiveness at being considered a dunce in school, has stung many a youth into a determination which has elevated him far above those who laughed at him, as in the case of newton, of adam clark, of sheridan, wellington, goldsmith, dr. chalmers, curran, disraeli, and hundreds of others. "whatever you wish, that you are; for such is the force of the human will, joined to the divine, that whatever we wish to be seriously, and with a true intention, that we become." while this is not strictly true, yet there is a deal of truth in it.

it is men like mirabeau, who "trample upon impossibilities;" like napoleon, who do not wait for opportunities, but make them; like grant, who has only "unconditional surrender" for the enemy, who change the very front of the world. "we have but what we make, and every good is locked by nature in a granite hand, sheer labor must unclench."

what cares henry l. bulwer for the suffocating cough, even though he can scarcely speak above a whisper? in the house of commons he makes his immortal speech on the irish church just the same.

"i can't, it is impossible," said a foiled lieutenant, to alexander. "be gone," shouted the conquering macedonian, "there is nothing impossible to him who will try."

were i called upon to express in a word the secret of so many failures among those who started out in life with high hopes, i should say unhesitatingly, they lacked will-power. they could not half will. what is a man without a will? he is like an engine without steam, a mere sport of chance, to be tossed about hither and thither, always at the mercy of those who have wills. i should call the strength of will the test of a young man's possibilities. can he will strong enough, and hold whatever he undertakes with an iron grip? it is the iron grip that takes the strong hold on life. what chance is there in this crowding, pushing, selfish, greedy world, where everything is pusher or pushed, for a young man with no will, no grip on life? "the truest wisdom," said napoleon, "is a resolute determination." an iron will without principle might produce a napoleon; but with character it would make a wellington or a grant, untarnished by ambition or avarice.

"the undivided will
't is that compels the elements and wrings
a human music from the indifferent air."

# CHAPTER IV.

## success under difficulties.

victories that are easy are cheap. those only are worth having which come as the result of hard fighting.--beecher.

man owes his growth chiefly to that active striving of the will, that encounter with difficulty, which we call effort; and it is astonishing to find how often results that seemed impracticable are thus made possible.--epes sargent.

i know no such unquestionable badge and ensign of a sovereign mind as that tenacity of purpose which, through all change of companions, or parties, or fortunes, changes never, bates no jot of heart or hope, but wearies out opposition and arrives at its port.--emerson.

yes, to this thought i hold with firm persistence;
the last result of wisdom stamps it true;
he only earns his freedom and existence
who daily conquers them anew.
goethe.

little minds are tamed and subdued by misfortunes; but great minds rise above them.--washington irving.

"i have here three teams that i want to get over to staten island," said a boy of twelve one day in 1806 to the innkeeper at south amboy, n. j. "if you will put us across, i'll leave with you one of my horses in pawn, and if i don't send you back six dollars within forty-eight hours you may keep the horse."

the innkeeper asked the reason for this novel proposition, and learned that the lad's father had contracted to get the cargo of a vessel stranded near sandy hook, and take it to new york in lighters. the boy had been sent with three wagons, six horses, and three men, to carry the cargo across a sand-spit to the lighters. the work accomplished, he had started with only six dollars to travel a long distance home over the jersey sands, and reached south amboy penniless. "i'll do it," said the innkeeper, as he looked into the bright honest eyes of the boy. the horse was soon redeemed.

* * * * * *

how can you keep a determined man from success: place stumbling-blocks in his way, and he uses them for stepping-stones. imprison him, and he produces the "pilgrim's progress." deprive him of eyesight, and he writes the "conquest of mexico."

* * * * * *

"my son," said this same boy's mother, on the first of may, 1810, when he asked her to lend him one hundred dollars to buy a boat, having imbibed a strong liking for the sea; "on the twenty-seventh of this month you will be sixteen years old. if, by that time, you will plow, harrow, and plant with corn the eight-acre lot, i will advance you the money." the field was rough and stony, but the work was done in time, and well done. from this small beginning cornelius vanderbilt laid the foundation of a colossal fortune. he would often work all night; and, as he was never absent from his post by day, he soon had the best business in new york harbor.

in 1813, when it was expected that new york would be attacked by british ships, all the boatmen except cornelius put in bids to convey provisions to the military posts around new york, naming extremely low rates, as the contractor would be exempted from military duty. "why don't you send in a bid?" asked his father. "of what use?" replied young vanderbilt; "they are offering to do the work at half price. it can't be done at such rates." "well," said his father, "it can do no harm to try for it." so, to please his father, but with no hope of success, cornelius made an offer fair to both sides, but did not go to hear the award. when his companions had all returned with long faces, he went to the commissary's office and asked if the contract had been given. "oh, yes," was the reply; "that business is settled. cornelius vanderbilt is the man. what?" he asked, seeing that the youth was apparently thunderstruck, "is it you?" "my name is cornelius vanderbilt," said the boatman. "well," said the commissary, "don't you know why we have given the contract to you?" "no." "why, it is because we want this business *done*, and we know you'll do it." character gives confidence.

in 1818 he owned two or three of the finest coasting schooners in new york harbor, and had a capital of nine thousand dollars. seeing that steam-vessels would soon win supremacy over those carrying sails only, he gave up his fine business to become the captain of a steamboat at one thousand dollars a year. for twelve years he ran between new york city and new brunswick, n. j. in 1829 he began business as a steamboat owner, in the face of opposition so bitter that he lost his last dollar. but the tide turned, and he prospered so rapidly that he at length owned over one hundred steamboats. he early identified himself with the growing railroad interests of the country, and became the richest man of his day in america.

barnum began the race of business life barefoot, for at the age of fifteen he was obliged to buy on credit the shoes he wore at his father's funeral. he was a remarkable example of success under difficulties. there was no keeping him down; no opposition daunted him, no obstacles were too great for him to overcome. think of a man being ruined at fifty years of age; yes, worse than ruined, for he was heavily in debt besides. yet on the very day of his downfall he begins to rise again, wringing victory from defeat by his indomitable persistence.

"eloquence must have been born with you," said a friend to j. p. curran. "indeed, my dear sir, it was not," replied the orator, "it was born some three and twenty years and some months after me." speaking of his first attempt at a debating club, he said: "i stood up, trembling through every fibre, but remembering that in this i was but imitating tully, i took courage and had actually proceeded almost as far as 'mr. chairman,' when, to my astonishment and terror, i perceived that every eye was turned on me. there were only six or seven present, and the room could not have contained as many more; yet was it, to my panic-stricken imagination, as if i were the central object in nature, and assembled millions were gazing upon me in breathless expectation. i became dismayed and dumb. my friends cried, 'hear him!' but there was nothing to hear." he was nicknamed "orator mum," and well did he deserve the title until he ventured to stare in astonishment at a speaker who was "culminating chronology by the most preposterous anachronisms." "i doubt not," said the annoyed speaker, "that 'orator mum' possesses wonderful talents for eloquence, but i would recommend him to show it in future by some more popular method than his silence." stung by the taunt, curran rose and gave the man a "piece of his mind," speaking quite fluently in his anger. encouraged by this success, he took great pains to become a good speaker. he corrected his habit of stuttering by reading favorite passages aloud every day slowly and distinctly, and spoke at every opportunity.

bunyan wrote his "pilgrim's progress" on the untwisted papers used to cork the bottles of milk brought for his meals. gifford wrote his first copy of a mathematical work, when a cobbler's apprentice, on small scraps of leather; and rittenhouse, the astronomer, first calculated eclipses on his plow handle.

a poor irish lad, so pitted by smallpox that boys made sport of him, earned his living by writing little ballads for street musicians. eight cents a day was often all he could earn. he traveled through france and italy, begging his way by singing and playing the flute at the cottages of the peasantry. at twenty-eight he was penniless in london, and lived in the beggars' quarters in axe lane. in his poverty, he set up as a doctor in the suburbs of london. he wore a second-hand coat of rusty velvet, with a patch on the left breast which he adroitly covered with his three-cornered hat during his visits; and we have an amusing anecdote of his contest of courtesy with a patient who persisted in endeavoring to relieve him of his hat, which only made him press it more devoutly to his heart. he often had to pawn his clothes to keep from starving. he sold his "life of voltaire" for twenty dollars. after great hardship he managed to publish his "polite learning in europe," and this brought him to public notice. next came "the traveller," and the wretched man in a fleet street garret found himself famous. his landlady once arrested him for rent, but dr. johnson came to his relief, took from his desk the manuscript of the "vicar of wakefield," and sold it for three hundred dollars. he spent two years revising "the deserted village" after it was first written. generous to a fault, vain and improvident, imposed on by others, he was continually in debt; although for his "history of the earth and animated nature" he received four thousand dollars, and some of his works, as, for instance, "she stoops to conquer," had a large sale. but in spite of fortune's frown and his own weakness, he won success and fame. the world, which so often comes too late with its assistance and laurels, gave to the weak, gentle, loving author of "the vicar of wakefield" a monument in the poets' corner of westminster abbey.

the poor, scrofulous, and almost blind boy, samuel johnson, was taken by his mother to receive the touch of queen anne, which was supposed to heal the "king's evil." he entered oxford as a servant, copying lectures from a student's notebooks, while the boys made sport of the bare feet showing through great holes in his shoes. some one left a pair of new shoes at his door, but he was too proud to be helped, and threw them out of the window. he was so poor that he was obliged to leave college, and at twenty-six married a widow of forty-eight. he started a private school with his wife's money; but, getting only three pupils, was obliged to close it. he went to london, where he lived on nine cents a day. in his distress he wrote a poem in which appeared in capital letters the line, "slow rises worth by poverty depressed," which attracted wide attention. he suffered greatly in london for thirteen years, being arrested once for a debt of thirteen dollars. at forty he published "the vanity of human wishes," in which were these lines:--

"then mark what ills the scholar's life assail;
toil, envy, want, the patron and the jail."

when asked how he felt about his failures, he replied:

"like a monument,"--that is, steadfast, immovable. he was an indefatigable worker. in the evenings of a single week he wrote "rasselas," a beautiful little story of the search for happiness, to get money to pay the funeral expenses of his mother. with six assistants he worked seven years on his dictionary, which made his fortune. his name was then in everybody's mouth, and when he no longer needed help, assistance, as usual, came from every quarter. the great universities hastened to bestow their degrees, and king george invited him to the palace.

lord mansfield raised himself by indefatigable industry from oatmeal porridge and poverty to affluence and the lord chief justice's bench.

of five thousand articles sent every year to "lippincott's magazine," only two hundred were accepted. how much do you think homer got for his iliad? or dante for his paradise? only bitter bread and salt, and going up and down other people's stairs. in science, the man who discovered the telescope, and first saw heaven, was paid with a dungeon: the man who invented the microscope, and first saw earth, died from starvation, driven from his home. it is very clear indeed that god means all good work and talk to be done for nothing. shakespeare's "hamlet" was sold for about twenty-five dollars; but his autograph has sold for five thousand dollars.

during the ten years in which he made his greatest discoveries, isaac newton could hardly pay two shillings a week to the royal society of which he was a member. some of his friends wanted to get him excused from this payment, but he would not allow them to act.

there are no more interesting pages in biography than those which record how emerson, as a child, was unable to read the second volume of a certain book, because his widowed mother could not afford the amount (five cents) necessary to obtain it from the circulating library.

linnaeus was so poor when getting his education, that he had to mend his shoes with folded paper, and often had to beg his meals of his friends.

who in the days of the first empire cared to recall the fact that napoleon, emperor and king, was once forced to borrow a louis from talma, when he lived in a garret on the quai conti?

david livingstone at ten years of age was put into a cotton factory near glasgow. out of his first week's wages he bought a latin grammar, and studied in the night schools for years. he would sit up and study till midnight unless his mother drove him to bed, notwithstanding he had to be at the factory at six in the morning. he mastered virgil and horace in this way, and read extensively, besides studying botany. so eager and thirsty for knowledge was he, that he would place his book before him on the spinning-jenny, and amid the deafening roar of machinery would pore over its pages.

george eliot said of the years of close work upon her "romola," "i began it a young woman, i finished it an old woman." one of emerson's biographers says, referring to his method of rewriting, revising, correcting, and eliminating: "his apples were sorted over and over again, until only the very rarest, the most perfect, were left. it did not matter that those thrown away were very good and helped to make clear the possibilities of the orchard, they were unmercifully cast aside." carlyle's books were literally wrung out of him. the pains he took to satisfy himself of a relatively insignificant fact were incredible. before writing his essay on diderot, he read twenty-five volumes at the rate of one per day. he tells edward fitzgerald that for the twentieth time he is going over the confused records of the battle of naseby, that he may be quite sure of the topography.

"all the performances of human art, at which we look with praise and wonder," says johnson, "are instances of the resistless force of perseverance: it is by this that the quarry becomes a pyramid, and that distant countries are united with canals. if a man was to compare the effect of a single stroke of the pickaxe, or of one impression of the spade, with the general design and last result, he would be overwhelmed by the sense of their disproportion; yet those petty operations, incessantly continued, in time surmount the greatest difficulties, and mountains are leveled, and oceans bounded, by the slender force of human beings."

the rev. eliphalet nott, a pulpit orator, was especially noted for a sermon on the death of alexander hamilton, the great statesman, who was shot in a duel by aaron burr. although nott had managed in some way to get his degree at brown university, he was at one time so poor after he entered the ministry that he could not buy an overcoat. his wife sheared their only cosset sheep in january, wrapped it in burlap blankets to keep it from freezing, carded and spun and wove the wool, and made it into an overcoat for him.

great men never wait for opportunities; they make them. nor do they wait for facilities or favoring circumstances; they seize upon whatever is at hand, work out their problem, and master the situation. a young man determined and willing will find a way or make one. a franklin does not require elaborate apparatus; he can bring electricity from the clouds with a common kite. a watt can make a model of the condensing steam-engine out of an old syringe used to inject the arteries of dead bodies previous to dissection. a dr. black can discover latent heat with a pan of water and two thermometers. a newton can unfold the composition of light and the origin of colors with a prism, a lens, and a piece of pasteboard. a humphry davy can experiment with kitchen pots and pans, and a faraday can experiment on electricity by means of old bottles, in his spare minutes while a book-binder. when science was in its cradle the marquis of worcester, an english nobleman, imprisoned in the tower of london, was certainly not in a very good position to do anything for the world, but would not waste his time. the cover of a vessel of hot water blown on before his eyes led to a series of observations, which he published later in a book called "century of inventions." these observations were a sort of text-book on the power of steam, which resulted in newcomen's steam-engine, which watt afterward perfected. a ferguson maps out the heavenly bodies, lying on his back, by means of threads with beads stretched between himself and the stars.

not in his day of bodily strength and political power, but blind, decrepit, and defeated with his party, milton composed "paradise lost."

great men have found no royal road to their triumph. it is always the old route, by way of industry and perseverance.

the farmer boy, elihu b. washburn, taught school at ten dollars per month, and early learned the lesson that it takes one hundred cents to make a dollar. in after years he fought "steals" in congress, until he was called the "watchdog of the treasury." from his long membership he became known as the "father of the house." he administered the oath to schuyler colfax as speaker three times. he recommended grant as colonel of a regiment of volunteers. the latter, when president, appointed him secretary of state, and, later, minister to france. during the reign of the commune, the representatives of nearly all other foreign nations fled in dismay, but washburn remained at his post. shells exploded close to his office, and fell all around it, but he did not leave even when paris was in flames. for a time he was really the minister of all foreign countries, in paris; and represented prussia for almost a year. the emperor william conferred upon him the order of the red eagle, and gave him a jeweled star of great value.

how could the poor boy, elihu burritt, working nearly all the daylight in a blacksmith's shop, get an education? he had but one book in his library, and carried that in his hat. but this boy with no chance became one of america's wonders.

when teaching school, garfield was very poor. he tore his only blue jean trousers, but concealed the rents by pins until night, when he retired early that his boarding mistress might mend his clothes. "when you get to be a united states senator," said she, "no one will ask what kind of clothes you wore when teaching school."

although michael angelo made himself immortal in three different occupations, his fame might well rest upon his dome of st. peter as an architect, upon his "moses" as a sculptor, and upon his "last judgment" as a painter; yet we find by his correspondence now in the british museum, that when he was at work on his colossal bronze statue of pope julius ii., he was so poor that he could not have his younger brother come to visit him at bologna, because he had but one bed in which he and three of his assistants slept together.

"i was always at the bottom of my purse," said zola, in describing the struggles of his early years of authorship. "very often i had not a sou left, and not knowing, either, where to get one. i rose generally at four in the morning, and began to study after a breakfast consisting of one raw egg. but no matter, those were good times. after taking a walk along the quays, i entered my garret, and joyfully partaking of a dinner of three apples, i sat down to work. i wrote, and i was happy. in winter i would allow myself no fire; wood was too expensive--only on fete days was i able to afford it. but i had several pipes of tobacco and a candle for three sous. a three-sous candle, only think of it! it meant a whole night of literature to me."

james brooks, once the editor and proprietor of the "new york daily express," and later an eminent congressman, began life as a clerk in a store in maine, and when twenty-one received for his pay a hogshead of new england rum. he was so eager to go to college that he started for waterville with his trunk on his back, and when he was graduated he was so poor and plucky that he carried his trunk on his back to the station when he went home.

when elias howe, harassed by want and woe, was in london completing his first sewing-machine, he had frequently to borrow money to live on. he bought beans and cooked them himself. he also borrowed money to send his wife back to america. he sold his first machine for five pounds, although it was worth fifty, and then he pawned his letters patent to pay his expenses home.

the boy arkwright begins barbering in a cellar, but dies worth a million and a half. the world treated his novelties just as it treats everybody's novelties--made infinite objection, mustered all the impediments, but he snapped his fingers at their objections, and lived to become honored and wealthy.

there is scarcely a great truth or doctrine but has had to fight its way to public recognition in the face of detraction, calumny, and persecution. "everywhere," says heine, "that a great soul gives utterance to its thoughts, there also is a golgotha."

nearly every great discovery or invention that has blessed mankind has had to fight its way to recognition, even against the opposition of the most progressive men.

even sir charles napier fiercely opposed the introduction of steam power into the royal navy. in the house of commons, he exclaimed, "mr. speaker, when we enter her majesty's naval service and face the chances of war, we go prepared to be hacked in pieces, to be riddled by bullets, or to be blown to bits by shot and shell; but mr. speaker, we do not go prepared to be boiled alive." he said this with tremendous emphasis.

"will any one explain how there can be a light without a wick?" asked a member of parliament, when william murdock, toward the close of the eighteenth century, said that coal gas would give a good light, and could be conveyed into buildings in pipes. "do you intend taking the dome of st. paul's for a gasometer?" was the sneering question of even the great scientist, humphry davy. walter scott ridiculed the idea of lighting london by "smoke," but he soon used it at abbotsford, and davy achieved one of his greatest triumphs by experimenting with gas until he had invented his safety lamp.

titian used to crush the flowers to get their color, and painted the white walls of his father's cottage in tyrol with all sorts of pictures, at which the mountaineers gazed in wonder.

"that boy will beat me one day," said an old painter as he watched a little fellow named michael angelo making drawings of pot and brushes, easel and stool, and other articles in the studio. the barefoot boy did persevere until he had overcome every difficulty and become a master of his art.

william h. prescott was a remarkable example of what a boy with "no chance" can do. while at college, he lost one eye by a hard piece of bread thrown during a "biscuit battle," then so common after meals; and, from sympathy, the other eye became almost useless. but the boy had pluck and determination, and would not lead a useless life. he set his heart upon being a historian, and turned all his energies in that direction. by the aid of others' eyes, he spent ten years studying before he even decided upon a particular theme for his first book. then he spent ten years more, poring over old archives and manuscripts, before he published his "ferdinand and isabella." what a lesson in his life for young men! what a rebuke to those who have thrown away their opportunities and wasted their lives!

"galileo with an opera-glass," said emerson, "discovered a more splendid series of celestial phenomena than any one since with the great telescopes. columbus found the new world in an undecked boat."

surroundings which men call unfavorable cannot prevent the unfolding of your powers. from the plain fields and lowlands of avon came the shakespearean genius which has charmed the world. from among the rock-ribbed hills of new hampshire sprang the greatest of american orators and statesmen, daniel webster. from the crowded ranks of toil, and homes to which luxury is a stranger, have often come the leaders and benefactors of our race. indeed, when christ came upon earth, his early abode was a place so poor and so much despised that men thought he could not be the christ, asking, in utter astonishment, "can any good thing come out of nazareth?"

"i once knew a little colored boy," said frederick douglass, "whose mother and father died when he was but six years old. he was a slave, and had no one to care for him. he slept on a dirt floor in a hovel, and in cold weather would crawl into a meal-bag head foremost, and leave his feet in the ashes to keep them warm. often he would roast an ear of corn and eat it to satisfy his hunger, and many times has he crawled under the barn or stable and secured eggs, which he would roast in the fire and eat. that boy did not wear pantaloons, as you do, but a tow-linen shirt. schools were unknown to him, and he learned to spell from an old webster's spelling-book, and to read and write from posters on cellar and barn doors, while boys and men would help him. he would then preach and speak, and soon became well known. he became presidential elector, united states marshal, united states recorder, united states diplomat, and accumulated some wealth. he wore broadcloth, and didn't have to divide crumbs with the dogs under the table. that boy was frederick douglass. what was possible for me is possible for you. don't think because you are colored you can't accomplish anything. strive earnestly to add to your knowledge. so long as you remain in ignorance, so long will you fail to command the respect of your fellow-men."

where shall we find an illustration more impressive than in abraham lincoln, whose life, career, and death might be chanted by a greek chorus as at once the prelude and the epilogue of the most imperial theme of modern times? born as lowly as the son of god, in a hovel; of what real parentage we know not, reared in penury, squalor, with no gleam of light, nor fair surrounding; a young manhood vexed by weird dreams and visions; with scarcely a natural grace; singularly awkward, ungainly even among the uncouth about him: it was reserved for this remarkable character, late in life, to be snatched from obscurity, raised to supreme command at a supreme moment, and intrusted with the destiny of a nation. the great leaders of his party were made to stand aside; the most experienced and accomplished men of the day, men like seward, and chase, and sumner, statesmen famous and trained, were sent to the rear, while this strange figure was brought by unseen hands to the front, and given the reins of power.

the story is told of a man in london deprived of both legs and arms, who managed to write with his mouth and perform other things so remarkable as to enable him to earn a fair living. he would lay certain sheets of paper together, pinning them at the corner to make them hold. then he would take a pen and write some verses; after which he would proceed to embellish the lines by many skillful flourishes. dropping the pen from his mouth, he would next take up a needle and thread, also with his mouth, thread the needle, and make several stitches. he also painted with a brush, and was in many other ways a wonderful man. instead of being a burden to his family he was the most important contributor to their welfare.

arthur cavanagh, m. p., was born without arms or legs, yet it is said that he was a good shot, a skillful fisherman and sailor, and one of the best cross country riders in ireland. he was a good conversationalist, and an able member of parliament. he ate with his fork attached to his stump of an arm, and wrote holding his pen in his teeth. in riding he held the bridle in his mouth, his body being strapped to the saddle. he once lost his means of support in india, but went to work with his accustomed energy, and obtained employment as a carrier of dispatches.

people thought it strange that gladstone should appoint blind henry fawcett postmaster-general of great britain; but never before did any one fill the office so well.

john b. herreshoff, of bristol, r. i., although blind since he was fifteen years old, is the founder and head of one of the most noted shipbuilding establishments in the world. he has superintended the construction of some of the swiftest torpedo boats and steam and sailing yachts afloat. he frequently takes his turn at the wheel in sailing his vessels on trial trips. he is aided greatly by his younger brother nathaniel, but can plan vessels and conduct business without him. after examining a vessel's hull or a good model of it, he will give detailed instructions for building another just like it, and will make a more accurate duplicate than can most boat-builders whose sight is perfect.

the rev. william h. milburn, who lost his sight when a child, studied for the ministry, and was ordained before he attained his majority. in ten years he traveled about 200,000 miles in missionary work. he has written half a dozen books, among them a very careful history of the mississippi valley. he has long been chaplain of the lower house of congress.

blind fanny crosby, of new york, was a teacher of the blind for many years. she has written nearly three thousand hymns, among which are "pass me not, o gentle saviour," "rescue the perishing," "saviour more than life to me," and "jesus keep me near the cross."

nor are these by any means the only examples of blind people now doing their full share of the world's work. in the united states alone there are engaged in musical occupation one hundred and fifty blind piano tuners, one hundred and fifty blind teachers of music in schools for the blind, five hundred blind private teachers, one hundred blind church organists, fifteen or more blind composers and publishers of music, and several blind dealers in musical instruments.

*there is no open door to the temple of success.* every one who enters makes his own door, which closes behind him to all others, not even permitting his own children to pass.

nearly forty years ago, on a rainy, dreary day in november, a young widow in philadelphia sat wondering how she could feed and clothe three little ones left dependent by the death of her husband, a naval officer. happening to think of a box of which her husband had spoken, she opened it, and found therein an envelope containing directions for a code of colored light signals to be used at night on the ocean. the system was not complete, but she perfected it, went to washington, and induced the secretary of the navy to give it a trial. an admiral soon wrote that the signals were good for nothing, although the idea was valuable. for months and years she worked, succeeding at last in producing brilliant lights of different colors. she was paid $20,000 for the right to manufacture them in our navy. nearly all the blockade runners captured in the civil war were taken by the aid of the coston signals, which are also considered invaluable in the life saving service. mrs. coston introduced them into several european navies, and became wealthy.

a modern writer says that it is one of the mysteries of our life that genius, that noblest gift of god to man, is nourished by poverty. its greatest works have been achieved by the sorrowing ones of the world in tears and despair. not in the brilliant salon, not in the tapestried library, not in ease and competence, is genius usually born and nurtured; but often in adversity and destitution, amidst the harassing cares of a straitened household, in bare and fireless garrets, with the noise of squalid children, in the turbulence of domestic contentions, and in the deep gloom of uncheered despair. this is its most frequent birthplace, and amid scenes like these unpropitious, repulsive, wretched surroundings, have men labored, studied, and trained themselves, until they have at last emanated from the gloom of that obscurity the shining lights of their times; have become the companions of kings, the guides and teachers of their kind, and exercised an influence upon the thought of the world amounting to a species of intellectual legislation.

chauncey jerome's education was limited to three months in the district school each year until he was ten, when his father took him into his blacksmith shop at plymouth, conn., to make nails. money was a scarce article with young chauncey. he once chopped a load of wood for one cent, and often chopped by moonlight for neighbors at less than a dime a load. his father died when he was eleven, and his mother was forced to send chauncey out, with tears in his eyes and a little bundle of clothes in his hand, to earn a living on a farm. his new employer kept him at work early and late chopping down trees all day, his shoes sometimes full of snow, for he had no boots until he was nearly twenty-one. at fourteen he was apprenticed for seven years to a carpenter, who gave him only board and clothes. several times during his apprenticeship he carried his tools thirty miles on his back to his work at different places. after he had learned his trade he frequently walked thirty miles to a job with his kit upon his back. one day he heard people talking of eli terry, of plymouth, who had undertaken to make two hundred clocks in one lot. "he'll never live long enough to finish them," said one. "if he should," said another, "he could not possibly sell so many. the very idea is ridiculous." chauncey pondered long over this rumor, for it had long been his dream to become a great clock-maker. he tried his hand at the first opportunity, and soon learned to make a wooden clock. when he got an order to make twelve at twelve dollars apiece he thought his fortune was made. one night he happened to think that a cheap clock could be made of brass as well as of wood, and would not shrink, swell, or warp appreciably in any climate. he acted on the idea, and became the first great manufacturer of brass clocks. he made millions at the rate of six hundred a day, exporting them to all parts of the globe.

"the history of the english people" was written while j. r. green was struggling against a mortal illness. he had collected a vast store of materials, and had begun to write, when his disease made a sudden and startling progress, and his physicians said they could do nothing to arrest it. in the extremity of ruin and defeat he applied himself with greater fidelity to his work. the time that might still be left to him for work must henceforth be wrested, day by day, from the grasp of death. the writing occupied five months, while from hour to hour and day to day his life was prolonged, his doctors said, by the sheer force of his own will and his inflexible determination to finish the "making of england." he lay, too weak to lift a book, or to hold a pen, dictating every word, sometimes through hours of intense suffering. yet so conscientious was he that, driven by death as he was, the greater part of the book was rewritten five times. when it was done he began the "conquest of england," wrote it, reviewed it, and then, dissatisfied with it, rejected it all and began again. as death laid its cold fingers on his heart, he said: "i still have some work to do that i know is good. i will try to win but one week more to write it down." it was not until he was actually dying that he said, "i can work no more."

"what does he know," said a sage, "who has not suffered?" schiller produced his greatest tragedies in the midst of physical suffering almost amounting to torture. handel was never greater than when, warned by palsy of the approach of death, and struggling with distress and suffering, he sat down to compose the great works which have made his name immortal in music. mozart composed his great operas, and last of all his "requiem," when oppressed by debt and struggling with a fatal disease. beethoven produced his greatest works amidst gloomy sorrow, when oppressed by almost total deafness.

perhaps no one ever battled harder to overcome obstacles which would have disheartened most men than demosthenes. he had such a weak voice, and such an impediment in his speech, and was so short of breath, that he could scarcely get through a single sentence without stopping to rest. all his first attempts were nearly drowned by the hisses, jeers, and scoffs of his audiences. his first effort that met with success was against his guardian, who had defrauded him, and whom he compelled to refund a part of his fortune. he was so discouraged by his defeats that he determined to give up forever all attempts at oratory. one of his auditors, however, believed the young man had something in him, and encouraged him to persevere. he accordingly appeared again in public, but was hissed down as before. as he withdrew, hanging his head in great confusion, a noted actor, satyrus, encouraged him still further to try to overcome his impediment. he stammered so much that he could not pronounce some of the letters at all, and his breath would give out before he could get through a sentence. finally, he determined to be an orator cost what it might. he went to the seashore and practiced amid the roar of the breakers with small pebbles in his mouth, in order to overcome his stammering, and at the same time accustom himself to the hisses and tumults of his audience. he overcame his short breath by practicing speaking while running up steep and difficult places on the shore. his awkward gestures were also corrected by long and determined drill before a mirror.

disheartened by the expense of removing the troublesome seeds, southern planters were seriously considering the abandonment of cotton culture. to clean a pound of cotton required the labor of a slave for a day. eli whitney, a young man from new england, teaching school in georgia, saw the state of affairs, and determined to invent a machine to do the work. he worked in secret for many months in a cellar, and at last made a machine which cleaned the cotton perfectly and rapidly. just as success crowned his long labor thieves broke into the cellar and stole his model. he recovered the model, but the principle was stolen, and other machines were made without his consent. in vain he tried to protect his right in the courts, for southern juries would almost invariably decide against him. he had started the south in a great industry, and added millions to her wealth, yet the courts united with the men who had infringed his patents to rob him of the reward of his ingenuity and industry. at last he abandoned the whole thing in disgust, and turned his attention to making improvements in firearms, and with such success that he accumulated a fortune.

robert collyer, who brought his bride in the steerage when he came to america at the age of twenty-seven, worked at the anvil nine years in pennsylvania, and then became a preacher, soon winning national renown.

a shrewd observer says of john chinaman: "no sooner does he put his foot among strangers than he begins to work. no office is too menial or too laborious for him. he has come to make money, and he will make it. his frugality requires but little: he barely lives, but he saves what he gets; commences trade in the smallest possible way, and is continually adding to his store. the native scorns such drudgery, and remains poor; the chinaman toils patiently on, and grows rich. a few years pass by, and he has warehouses; becomes a contractor for produce; buys foreign goods by the cargo; and employs his newly imported countrymen, who have come to seek their fortune as he did. he is not particularly scrupulous in matters of opinion. he never meddles with politics, for they are dangerous and not profitable; but he will adopt any creed, and carefully follow any observances, if, by so doing, he can confirm or improve his position. he thrives with the spaniard, and works while the latter sleeps. he is too quick for the dutchman, and can smoke and bargain at the same time. he has harder work with the englishman, but still he is too much for him, and succeeds. climate has no effect on him: it cannot stop his hands, unless it kills him; and if it does, he dies in harness, battling for money till his last breath. whoever he may be, and in whatever position, whether in his own or a foreign country, he is diligent, temperate, and uncomplaining. he keeps the word he pledges, pays his debts, and is capable of noble and generous actions. it has been customary to speak lightly of him, and to judge a whole people by a few vagabonds in a provincial seaport, whose morals and manners have not been improved by foreign society."

columbus was dismissed as a fool from court after court, but he pushed his suit against an incredulous and ridiculing world. rebuffed by kings, scorned by queens, he did not swerve a hair's breadth from the overmastering purpose which dominated his soul. the words "new world" were graven upon his heart; and reputation, ease, pleasure, position, life itself if need be, must be sacrificed. threats, ridicule, ostracism, storms, leaky vessels, mutiny of sailors, could not shake his mighty purpose.

you cannot keep a determined man from success. place stumbling-blocks in his way and he takes them for stepping-stones, and on them will climb to greatness. take away his money, and he makes spurs of his poverty to urge him on. cripple him, and he writes the waverley novels. lock him up in a dungeon, and he composes the immortal "pilgrim's progress." put him in a cradle in a log cabin in the wilderness of america, and in a few years you will find him in the capitol at the head of the greatest nation on the globe.

would it were possible to convince the struggling youth of to-day that all that is great and noble and true in the history of the world is the result of infinite pains-taking, perpetual plodding, of common every-day industry!

when lavoisier the chemist asked that his execution might be postponed for a few days in order to ascertain the results of the experiments he was conducting in prison, the communists refused to grant the request, saying: "the republic has no need of philosophers." dr. priestley's house was burned and his chemical library destroyed by a mob shouting: "no philosophers," and he was forced to flee from his country. bruno

Made in the USA
Columbia, SC
12 November 2023

26065078R00037